It's Our Turn

Carrying on
the Work of the Pioneers
of Catholic Education
in Ontario

Mark G. McGowan

NOVALIS

For my parents,

Douglas Gillan McGowan (1933–1973)
& Elizabeth Anne Giesler (1934–2017)

Tireless supporters of Catholic education

© 2019 Novalis Publishing Inc.

Cover design: Martin Gould
Cover image: Getty Images
Layout: Audrey Wells

Published by Novalis

Publishing Office
1 Eglinton Avenue East, Suite 800
Toronto, Ontario, Canada
M4P 3A1

Head Office
4475 Frontenac Street
Montréal, Québec, Canada
H2H 2S2

www.novalis.ca

Library and Archives Canada Cataloguing in Publication

McGowan, Mark George, 1959-, author
    It's our turn : carrying on the work of the pioneers
of Catholic education in Ontario / Mark McGowan.

ISBN 978-2-89688-563-3 (softcover)

    1. Catholic schools--Ontario. 2. Catholic schools--Ontario--
History. I. Title.

LC504.2.O5M34 2019   371.071'2713   C2018-905040-3

Printed in Canada.

We acknowledge the support of the Government of Canada.

5 4 3 2 1   23   22   21   20   19

Table of Contents

Acknowledgements 5

Preface 8

Introduction 9

The History of Catholic Schools in Ontario: An Overview 20

1. Bishop Jean-Olivier Briand: Prudence and the Art
   of the Possible 35

2. Bishop Michael Power: Moderation and Determination 39

3. Mother Teresa Dease, IBVM: Gentle Fortitude 44

4. Bishop Armand-François-Marie de Charbonnel:
   Tireless Advocate 49

5. Sister Bernard Dinan, CSJ: Patience and Perseverance 54

6. Sir Richard William Scott: One Who Thirsted for Justice 58

7. Thomas D'Arcy McGee: Eloquent Advocate 63

8. Archbishop John Joseph Lynch: Diplomacy, Advocacy,
   and Controversy 67

9. James Francis White: Devotion to Duty 72

10. Bishop Michael Francis Fallon, OMI: Controversial Crusader .. 77

11. Napoléon-Antoine Belcourt: Language Guardian of the Faith... 82

12. Father John Joseph O'Gorman: Priest, Educator, and Padre 88

13. Mary Margaret Eleanor Williams
(Mother Mary Genevieve, OSU): Teacher of Teachers 92

14. John Read Teefy, CSB: Catholic School Visionary 97

15. Archbishop Neil McNeil: Prophetic Voice for Justice 102

16. Martin Joseph Quinn: Passionate Lay Leadership 107

17. Margaret Lynch: Teacher and Labour Advocate 112

18. Bartley Edmund "Ed" Nelligan: Architect of a New Era 117

19. Anna Clare Berrigan, GSIC, Father Leo Austin, and Desmond
Newman: Building Clerical, Lay, and Religious Partnerships—
The Founding of Denis O'Connor Catholic Secondary School,
Whitby 124

20. Lorne Howcroft: Principled Principal 129

Afterword 135

Selected Bibliography 139

Index 147

Acknowledgements

This unanticipated little book has been the result of many years of my toiling on small projects exploring the publicly funded Catholic school systems of Canada. My work has been facilitated by many people, both past and present. First and foremost, I would like to thank Dr. Robert Dixon, who engaged me as an historical advisor on the Ontario English Catholic Teachers' Association (OECTA) challenge to Bill 104, the first of the Ontario government's attempts to restructure education. Although Bob left the project, Paul Cavalluzzo, OECTA's chief legal counsel, helped shepherd my affidavit, which had turned into a serious historical re-examination of separate school taxation in Ontario. This work came to the attention of Carol Devine who, on behalf of the Ontario Catholic School Trustees' Association, asked me to write a short history of Catholic education that could be easily consumed by a non-academic audience. Her guidance and support were invaluable; the result was *The Enduring Gift*, which has been edited and revised many times since it first appeared in 1997.

I am also in the debt of two directors of the Institute for Catholic Education (ICE): Sister Joan Cronin, GSIC, who has been an unfailing supporter and promoter of my academic work on Catholic education; and Michael Pautler, who has continued to invite me to share the story of Catholic education with Module D of the Supervisory Officer's Qualification Program (SOQP). The members of the Northern Ontario Catholic Curriculum Cooperative transformed *The Enduring Gift* into a short film and allowed me further opportunities to tell the story in a different medium. For this I am thankful. Likewise, my gratitude extends to Theresa Harris and the Ontario Catholic Supervisory Officers' Association (OCSOA), who in 2011 asked me to revise and update *The Enduring Gift* and produced a new film to accompany it. Now a revised version of the story can help teacher candidates understand a system in which they aspire to teach.

My friend and colleague Lou Rocha, formerly of the Catholic Principals' Council of Ontario (CPCO), repeatedly invited me to write a column in its magazine, *Principal Connections*, but my duties as Principal of St. Michael's College, University of Toronto, never allowed me much time to undertake anything outside my academic and administrative responsibilities. I want to extend my heartfelt apologies to Lou, but offer my thanks to him, nevertheless, for never holding this refusal against me. Years later, when I saw my administrative duties diminishing, Nelly Kelders of CPCO invited me to produce short biographies of selected pioneers of Catholic education for the magazine; these profiles now form the corpus of this book. My thanks to Nelly, Deirdre Kinsella Biss, and their staff at *Principal Connections* for helping bring this project to life.

So many labourers in the vineyard of Catholic education have taken time to help me, there are probably not enough pages in the book to list them all. Some have never refused my questions and have encouraged my work, so I reserve special thanks to my mentor, the late Peter Daly of Ottawa, and a host of leaders past and present in Catholic education: Noel Martin, James Mulligan, CSC, Yvonne Benton, Marcello Bottiglia, Brian Finamore, Dr. Brian O'Sullivan, Professor Elizabeth Smyth, Professor Peter Meehan, Michael Power, Sister Anna Clare Berrigan, GSIC, Desmond Newman, Frank Kavanaugh, OMI, the Hon. Sean Conway, Paul Reale, Bronek Korczynsky, Charlotte Lahey, Margaret Shea-Lawrence, Michael Baine, Tom Reilly, Sharon Grogan-Sheahan, Katie Shewfelt (of the Catholic Schools of Whitehorse), and directors of education, past and present, from Kenora to Kemptville, who have made me welcome in their boards and allowed me to share parts of their story with them. My wife, Eileen, who is a chaplain in a Catholic secondary school, shared valuable on-the-ground insights with me about the changing character of the stakeholders in the system, insights I found particularly valuable when I served for a short time as a trustee for the Durham Catholic District School Board. I also want to thank the archivists who have helped me over the years, including Marc Lerman, formerly at the Archives of the Archdiocese of Toronto; Sister Juliana Dusel, at the Loretto Sisters Archives; Sister Mary Ruddy, GSIC, of the Grey Sisters Archives in Pembroke; and Linda Wicks at the Archives of the Congregation of the Sisters of St. Joseph in Toronto.

Finally, I owe a special thanks to Joe Sinasac and Simon Appolloni of Novalis, who thought that reproducing the biographies, in addition to a revised *Enduring Gift*, might be a practical way of telling important parts of the story of Catholic education in Ontario at a time when the story risks being forgotten. As always, I am indebted to Anne Louise Mahoney, whose perspicacious eye and intellectual insight have made this book far superior to the unedited manuscript.

This book is dedicated to my parents, Doug and Betty Anne McGowan (nee Giesler), who spent much of their adult lives promoting and serving the cause of Catholic education. In the 1950s, while working as a director at CKNX Television in Wingham, Ontario, my father canvassed door to door to secure the needed ratepayers to found a separate school. In a rural county as "orange" as Huron, this young Catholic from Toronto was often met with heated opposition on the doorstep. This did not deter him from trying to exercise his constitutional rights secured by the British North America Act. My parents served on parent-teacher associations, worked on school advisory boards, and ran special events at a time when fundraising was constantly needed for separate schools, which always appeared to be in fragile condition monetarily and materially. Like most pioneers of Catholic education, their role is unsung, but without their small but meaningful contributions, and the tireless sacrifice of tens of thousands of parents like them, Catholic schools would not have survived in Ontario.

Preface

This book is intended as a primer in telling the story of Catholic schools in the province. It is designed as a quick read for busy people. It also aims to tell the story of Ontario's Catholic schools through the eyes and actions of those who lived it. As a culture, we are fascinated with biography, which remains one of the most popular genres in books, on television, and on the internet. So-called reality television has demonstrated, by its prolonged success and multiple story arcs (from the absurd to the ridiculous), how eager we are to engage in the messiness of other people's lives.

While the short biographies presented in this book are not the salacious and exaggerated profiles featured on popular reality shows, they are real stories of faith-filled people who often laid their lives on the line for Catholic education. Readers may find it fascinating to see how Catholic education was lived by the men and women who built schools, created curriculum, fought political battles, or humbled themselves for the sake of Catholic education. All of the persons represented in the profiles shared a deep Catholic faith and could not imagine a system of education that did not have faith formation and Christian witness at its heart. They all believed that a truly holistic education included educating the mind, the body, and the soul. The Introduction that follows maps out the urgency, in our own time, to remember the story and the pioneers of Catholic education who never forgot its importance to the Catholic community in Ontario.

Introduction

How the Story of Catholic Schools Was Lost (and How Today's Teachers, Parents, and Students Can Reclaim It)

n February 2018, *The Globe and Mail*, Canada's self-proclaimed national newspaper, published the results of a study it had undertaken to assess how many non-Catholic students were attending Ontario's publicly funded Catholic elementary schools.[1] Provisions of Bill 30, which in 1986 enacted funding completion to the end of high school, promised open access to all students in the new model of Catholic secondary schools. Such was not the case in elementary schools, where local boards made decisions on an *ad hoc* basis as to whether to allow non-Catholic students to register.

While many Catholic school boards had allowed non-Catholic students to become members of their school communities, the historic principle had essentially been that Catholic schools were for Catholic children, whose parents had to provide proof of Catholicity by an official baptismal certificate. The *Globe* report argued that by admitting non-Catholic students, Catholic school boards were threatening the enrolments in local public non-denominational schools, and as such should be reined in by the provincial government and cease the practice.

---

1   *The Globe and Mail*, February 10, 2018. A month later, an op-ed piece in the *Toronto Star* cited this enrolment study in its own call for the end of publicly funded Catholic schools. *Toronto Star*, March 13, 2018.

I suspect the *Globe* had been curious about this access question because of a similar situation in Saskatchewan, in which Catholic schools were taken to task for the same practice, because of serious underenrolments in some public school districts. The Government of Saskatchewan refused to stop Catholic school districts from allowing non-Catholics to attend their schools, citing long-standing precedents for such activity in the province and, therefore, a lack of willingness by the government to disrupt a practice that was essentially not creating the disaster alleged by supporters of public schools. When the government faced a constitutional challenge, they hinted simply that they might invoke the "notwithstanding clause" of the Constitution Act and thereby continue the practice despite court sanction.

Once again, the existence and activities of publicly funded Catholic schools in Canada were facing scrutiny and public opposition. Such controversy has generally been the fate of Catholic schools since the early 19th century. Born of a need to educate the whole child (physical, intellectual, spiritual), to keep the religious peace and protect Catholic children from proselytism, and to honour collective rights of religious minorities, Catholic schools have courted controversy and sometimes violent opposition since their inception. At each moment of crisis, there were always Catholic individuals and groups who stepped into the breach and used their creativity, political intelligence, and persuasive argument to keep opponents at bay and develop what was once called the "separate school" system in Ontario.

These Catholics were inspirational bishops, committed priests and women religious, and energetic laypersons who were able to navigate Catholic schools through political storms and the shoals of educational policy and, at times, bigotry. These Catholics were also well aware of the principles at stake in protecting and maintaining Catholic schools and often sacrificed money, time, friendships, and careers to keep the system afloat. In many of these moments of challenge, Catholic school ratepayers were witnesses to remarkable leaders who demonstrated creativity, vision, and passion as they made certain that the hard-fought rights secured at the time of Confederation were neither squandered nor allowed to stagnate in a rapidly changing social, educational, cultural, and religious environment in Ontario.

In 1984, and with the announcement of funding completion for Catholic schools from junior kindergarten to grade 13, the character of the struggle for Catholic education began to change. By the end of the decade, Catholic secondary schools, once the impoverished weak link of the separate school system, were receiving provincial funding, school boards were erecting state-of-the-art buildings for grades 9 to 13, and Catholic students no longer had to face paying tuition for their senior grades. In the 1990s, with full funding offered by the provincial government, Catholic school boards were now consolidated into larger units and fully funded from the public purse. For a variety of reasons, some of which were rooted in the parsimony of the specific government of the day, teachers were permitted to retire with pension once they had attained their "85 factor," a retirement age determined when the sum of their age and years in teaching equalled 85.

For weary teachers and administrators who had long suffered massive curricular changes that came as Queen's Park changed hands between Progressive Conservative, Liberal, and New Democratic Party regimes, and the politicization of education that often accompanied such shifts, the "85 factor" appeared as a blessed relief. Over time, however, it quickly removed the veterans of Catholic education from the scene, eliminating those who had been stewards of the story of struggle that had characterized the growth and survival of Catholic schools in the province. The story of Catholic schools was being lost. In a system that, within a generation, became state of the art, lacking for little materially, it is not surprising that at least one commentator saw Catholics as suffering from a "severe case of religious amnesia" and suggesting that in accepting funding completion, the Catholic community had drunk from a "poisoned chalice."[2]

The changing character of the Catholic Church has also added to the complexity of the challenges facing Catholic schools in the province. The Second Vatican Council (1962–1965) created a culture of updating across the Catholic world, including a significant transformation of the liturgy into the vernacular languages. The Church was seen less as institution, or through the lenses of a hierarchy, than as a community in which all—

---

2   Dennis Murphy, *Catholic Education at the Crossroads* (Toronto: *The Catholic Register*, 2001), 1 and 7.

clerical or lay—shared a common baptism as prophets, priests and kings, and thereby were co-responsible for the life and health of the Church.

Documents such as *Gaudium et Spes*, the Pastoral Constitution on the Church and the Modern World, called for the engagement of the Church with the secular world and encouraged lay leadership in the life of the Church, which itself had been redefined as the "people of God." The breaking down of these barriers also included documents that encouraged Catholics to engage in ecumenical dialogue with other Christians and in interfaith dialogue with the major non-Christian religions of the globe.[3]

Christian mission was now considered less a matter of proselytization and indoctrination, and more an emphasis on the missionary to bear witness to the Gospel by his or her actions in the field. With the Council came a rethinking of Catholic curriculum, away from traditional rote question-and-answer catechetics and towards a more child-centred and culturally sensitive means of teaching and embracing the Gospel. Catholic religious education, Catholic teachers, and the character of Catholic schools would change in the aftermath of the Council.

Not all Catholics were pleased with the outcomes of the Council or by the manner in which the Council was interpreted by clerical leaders over the next 50 years. Principles of episcopal collegiality and lay leadership have been interpreted variously since the Council, with a struggle developing between those who favour more centralized control over the institution and those who prefer a decentralized model of Church in which greater subsidiarity is witnessed in local and national churches throughout the Catholic world.

The Church has also encountered division over its pronouncements on sexuality, marriage, family life, and social justice. Many Catholics simply ignore the encyclical *Humanae Vitae* (1968) which prohibited Catholics from using artificial methods of birth control.[4] There have even been movements resistant to the vernacular liturgies introduced by the Council, with a minority of Catholics preferring a return not just to Latin, but to the form of liturgy put in place by the Council of Trent in the 16th century.

---

3   Austin Flannery, OP, ed., *The Documents of Vatican II* (New York: Pillar Books, 1975).

4   *The Tablet*, July 26, 2008.

Most recently, the Church internationally has faced warranted criticism for its mishandling of multiple cases of sexual abuse of children by clergy. The credibility of Church leaders has been called into question; Catholics are leaving the Church, feeling betrayed and ashamed. In our own times, the most powerful leaders in the Church are being challenged from within. The reformist and pastorally focused Pope Francis has been openly opposed by some of his cardinals on his pronouncements on faith, morality, and social ethics. While the opposition does not take up the violence and vehemence that factions of cardinals used against the Renaissance popes, fearlessness is revealed in the dissent expressed in Rome, and even Canada, against Francis's actions.[5] This open conflict, amplified in an age of mass communication and social media, has few precedents in the history of the modern papacy. Given even a cursory knowledge of Church history, one cannot help but lament what could happen to a Church divided.

These changes and challenges witnessed in the Catholic Church in the past fifty years have coincided with the rapid secularization of the Province of Ontario. Since the 1960s there has been a mass exodus from the Christian churches in Ontario. In their recent analysis of Canadian churches, titled *Leaving Christianity*, University of Toronto professors Brian P. Clarke and Stuart Macdonald have analyzed the deep crisis in Church affiliation and attendance across Canada from 1971 to 2011. The former bastions of Ontario Protestantism—mainstream churches such as the Anglican, United, and Presbyterian—have witnessed their number of adherents dwindle and church attendance reach new lows below 20 per cent. Roman Catholics have not been immune to this decline. In Quebec, the regular attendance of Catholics in liturgy sits at 10 per cent, and in the rest of Canada, it is around 25 per cent.

Canadians claiming affiliation to the Catholic Church are falling with each census, particularly among youth under 14 years of age and those millennials and post–baby boomers in the 25 to 45 age group.[6] Such decline does not bode well for the health of the Church as these generations age. In the past, the Catholic Church could rely on replenishment

---

5   *The Tablet*, January 6, 2018.

6   Brian P. Clarke and Stuart Macdonald, *Leaving Christianity: Changing Allegiances in Christianity since 1945* (Montreal & Kingston: McGill-Queen's University Press, 2017), 122–62.

from tens of thousands of Catholic immigrants, but this is no longer the case, as newcomers are now primarily from places in the world where Catholics are not numerous (India, Southeast Asia, the Middle East), except for the Philippines and Latin America. Moreover, almost a quarter of Canadians in 2011 declared they had "no religion," and as many as a third claimed no formal religious affiliation.[7]

In this more culturally diverse and secular Ontario, Catholic schools may be the only presence of Church that nominally Catholic children have. In some respects, the health of the Church in Ontario will greatly depend on the health of Catholic schools and the new generations of Catholics that will emerge from them. Knowing the story of these schools, the principles upon which they stand, their pioneers, and the sacrifices made in the past ought to bring greater awareness of how important these schools are for a faith community in very fragile times.

In part because of these dramatic changes taking place within the Catholic schools system and in the world that surrounds it, the Ontario Catholic School Trustees' Association asked me to write a short pamphlet to offer a concise version of the "story" of Catholic education that they thought was being lost. Years later, the trustees commissioned my friend and colleague Michael Power to write a full-length version, published as *The Promise Fulfilled*, to offer greater depth and detail to those who wanted to explore the story further.

Trustees were not alone in their concern that the story was being lost within the Catholic educational community, and perhaps with it knowledge of the legal, historical, and constitutional evidence traditionally marshalled in defence of Catholic education. School board directors of education, parents' groups, individual schools, Catholic teacher training programs, and business officers invited me to give a variety of talks on "the story" to kindle interest in a new generation of parents, teachers, and administrators who had little sense of the history of their school system or the principles upon which it stood.

---

7   Clarke and Macdonald, *Leaving Christianity*, 7, 166 and 187–90. In Ontario, those claiming No Religion, in 2011, was 23.8%. Note also Warren Clark and Grant Schellenberg, "Who's Religious," *Canadian Social Trends* (Summer 2006), 1–8.

As I crisscrossed the province and visited most of Ontario's Catholic district school boards, I became increasingly aware that the story and values for which Catholic education was based had become lost, or at best a faded memory. New generations of teachers, parents, and administrators, because of their age, and the greater financial and material comfort within the system since 1986, had lost a sense of the story; worse still, the stewards of the story and those who had lived the more recent chapters of it were retiring in droves, or were passing from this life.

The great danger has become that in this noisy world in which we are bombarded by information, misinformation, "fake news," and competing value systems, it has become easy to forget or ignore the *raison d'être* for Catholic schools and their evolution in Ontario. Memories must be rekindled; amnesia cured; and comfort and complacency with the status quo addressed in a meaningful way.

These latter points were presented to me vividly after one such presentation to students in a Catholic leadership seminar held at St. Michael's College (University of Toronto) in 1998. After having offered a lecture on the bare bones of the development of Ontario's Catholic schools, I was fielding questions in the Q&A session that invariably is more interesting than any of my talks. I was not disappointed. With a lull in the interrogation, a mature student put up her hand, was acknowledged, and began to tell her own story.

She was a recently minted doctoral student from the Faculty of Theology at St. Mike's and had been a teacher in her native Newfoundland and Labrador. She did not have a question, just a comment to the audience. She instructed them to listen and remember this story. She confessed that her fellow Newfoundland Catholics in a referendum on schools (in the end, two referenda) forgot their story, could not account for why and how their Catholic schools had come to be, and lost both a good hearing in the court of public opinion and ultimately the schools themselves.

The government of the province eventually eliminated all faith-based schools, replacing them with one publicly funded non-denominational system. The federal government refused to undertake its option of disallowance under Section 93 of the Constitution Act (which covered Newfoundland under Term 17 of the dominion joining Canada) and the provincial legislation stood uncontested. One could hear a pin drop in the room. Ontarians had been warned. Lose the story and a sense of one's Catholic identity and the same could happen to their schools if they cannot account for themselves when challenged by government or other groups in civil society.[8]

This book tells the story of 22 pioneers of Catholic education who never lost a sense of why Catholic education existed and of its importance to Catholics living in Ontario. While the profiles in the book are arranged in a rough chronological order, the book is also designed so that no one need read all of the profiles in sequence to get a sense of those profiles that follow. Each biography can be read as a self-contained study. In addition, unlike much of my previous academic writing, I have eliminated most footnotes in this book in an effort to create a flow in each chapter, with as few interruptions to the reader as possible. Each chapter, however, concludes with a short list of additional readings on the profiled subject and his/her context, if a reader wishes to delve deeper into a story. Similarly, this book concludes with a longer reading list to facilitate further research into the history of Catholic schools in Ontario.

There may be some consternation about the choice of the 22 "pioneers" of Catholic education in Ontario. The inclusion of Bishop Jean-Olivier Briand might shock some people. Briand never ventured to the territory that would become Ontario, even though it was part of his diocese, and likely would never have imagined the long-term implications of his abilities to have the Catholic faith accorded legal rights in his "conquered colony."

The element of surprise in the selections is deliberate. In understanding Bishop Briand, the reader may come to realize that the collective rights accorded the Catholic people of Ontario have deep roots elsewhere in colonial Canada. The Bishop of Quebec's co-operation with the British Protestant Crown would enable Catholics in the central Canadian colonies to enjoy political and social rights not enjoyed in most other places within the British Empire. Thus, the addition of Briand to this group represents an effort to include key historical figures that might be ignored

---

8 Bonaventure Fagan, *Trial: The Loss of Constitutional Rights in Education in Newfoundland and Labrador* (St. John's: ADDA Press, 2004). Fagan demonstrates clearly that Catholics did take a stand to save their schools, but in the end, failed.

in telling the story of Ontario's Catholic schools. So the first rule of thumb in selecting sketches for this volume was to imagine key figures locally, provincially, and nationally whose impact might easily be overlooked by those interested in the roots of Catholic education.

Most of the selections in the book are from the 19th and early 20th centuries, when the foundations and frameworks of Catholic education were laid. In a period of funding completion, post 1984, and finally full funding, in 1997, the architects of the pre-existing separate school system are the easiest to forget. An effort has been made to capture those who were influential both at the level of policy and politics, as well as those who dedicated their energies to improving pedagogy, curriculum, and life in the classroom.

Readers will note that in the early period of the history of the schools, most of the profiles are of bishops, clergy, and men and women belonging to religious orders. Aside from the fact that few laypersons engaged in Catholic schools left a detailed written record of their actions for future generations to appreciate, the simple historical fact is that clergy and religious were the dominant and recognized forces in Catholic education until the early 20th century. Bishops and priests served as public advocates for the system and as skilled negotiators in affecting legislative changes that would improve Catholic schools. Men's and women's religious orders were the backbone of the teaching cadre in the schools, and also had skills in curriculum design, pedagogical innovation, and effective institutional management. It stands to reason that many of the profiles in this book would reflect the dominant presence of clergy and religious in the first century of Ontario's Catholic schools.

This having been said, every effort was made to include those leading laymen who made significant contributions, whether it be Thomas D'Arcy McGee in political negotiations, or James Francis White, who insisted on curricular changes to meet the needs of modern Canada, or Martin J. Quinn, who provided Catholic laypersons with a strong voice in advocating fair taxation for Catholic schools. Since the profiles move in roughly a chronological order, more laypersons emerge in the latter chapters of the book, reflecting the fact that after 1945, the entire system was in transition from clerical dominance to lay leadership both in the classrooms and in the board rooms.

It should also be noted that whenever possible, notable women appear in profiles, despite the fact that religious orders often discouraged one member standing out prominently apart from her community. The four women religious featured in profiles also reflect four of the dominant religious orders of women who undertook the building and development of Catholic schools in the province: the Institute of the Blessed Virgin Mary (Loretto Sisters); the Congregation of the Sisters of St. Joseph; the Grey Sisters of the Immaculate Conception; and the Ursuline Sisters. While dozens of religious orders engaged in the Catholic educational project in the province, these four orders were among the most prominent in their numbers of teachers, their rootedness in the history of the Church in the province, and their geographical dispersion.

The profiles of these sisters cover a variety of regions of the province from Chatham to Pembroke, as this book tries to capture local stories of Catholic education, thereby avoiding the oft-observed tendency to focus too much on Toronto. While there certainly has been much written on education focused on Toronto, and Catholic leaders invariably found themselves working in Toronto because it was the seat of the provincial government and the Department of Education, this book endeavours to look beyond Toronto to witness how Catholic education was experienced in other parts of the province.

No doubt some readers will be disappointed that so many pioneers of Catholic education have not received formal recognition in this book. It is likely that it would take a much larger book to tell the stories of the hundreds of Catholics, clergy, religious, and lay, who gave so much of their time and talent to build and improve Catholic schools in Ontario. I would hope that this book might inspire others to tell the stories of the many other pioneers of Catholic education who are excluded from these pages. All of the individuals featured in this book, except two included in the chapter on Whitby,[9] have met their eternal reward. Only deceased pioneers were included for several reasons: the need of good

---

9   Desmond Newman and Sister Anna Clare Berrigan, GSIC, were very much alive when this book
     went to press.

documentation to chronicle their lives and the need of some distance in order to acquire some perspective on how their lives could be placed within their proper context, in an effort to articulate their contributions accurately, insightfully, and dispassionately. To this end, the biographies are preceded by a concise overview of the history of Catholic schools in Ontario, so that a context can be set for these lives lived.

The History of Catholic Schools in Ontario

An Overview

Foundations

The first pioneers in what was then called Upper Canada never antici-pated the creation of a state-supported, universally accessible, and comprehensive Catholic education system in Ontario. In the 1830s, Catholic education—for that matter, any education—was considered to be within the realm of the few young men training for the Church, pub-lic service, or the professions. Bishop Alexander Macdonell of Kingston secured some financial support from the Crown for schoolmasters, some of whom were his priests. Small groups of children undertook a classical and catechetical education in their parish rectory, in a local home, or in log schoolhouses often shared between Catholics and their non-Catholic neighbours.

In 1841, Macdonell's dream of more permanent funding for Catholic schools by the State was partially realized, when the new School Act for the United Province of Canada (a union of Upper and Lower Canada, today's Ontario and Quebec) included a clause that permitted Catholics and others to establish denominational schools. The growth of Catholic schools over the next 25 years was punctuated by sectarian violence, linguistic conflict, and political maneuvering within the poorly con-ceived and constitutionally flawed legislature of Canada. These schools also emerged at a time in the 1840s and 1850s when Egerton Ryerson, the school superintendent of Canada West, pushed for a free, universal, and academically progressive public school system in Upper Canada. He believed such schools would promote loyalty to the Crown, solid citizenship, a sound curriculum, and a generic Christianity.

The latter point was troubling to many Catholics, who believed that the nonsectarian Christianity promoted in public schools, and fostered by the large numbers of Protestant schoolmasters, amounted to little more than Protestant proselytization. Bishop Armand de Charbonnel of Toronto (1850–1860) went so far as to call public schools an "insult" to the Catholic population: he urged his flock to establish and support distinctively Catholic schools. All of this squabbling over education came at a time of troubled relations between Catholics and Protestants in Canada. Although these were caused, in part, by sectarian bitterness imported from Europe, Upper Canadian Christians created their own reasons to prey upon one another: the arrival of thousands of Irish Catholic refugees from the potato famine was regarded as a scourge upon the land, while French Canadian Catholic legislators were accused of furthering the interests of Catholicism by means of their strong presence in the Legislative Assembly. In the 1850s, expressions of sectarian bitterness varied from hateful rhetorical exchanges between Protestants and Catholics in the public press to full-fledged riots in the towns and cities of Ontario.

The Taché Act and the Scott Act

The extension of Catholic schools in Upper Canada was often at the heart of the bitterness and bloodshed. In 1855, by the weight of French Canadian Catholic votes, the Assembly passed the Taché Act, which extended the rights of Upper Canada's Catholic minority to create and manage their own schools. Similarly, in 1863, the votes of French Canadian Catholic legislators and their moderate Anglophone allies passed the Scott Act, which, among other things, confirmed that Catholic school trustees possessed the same rights and privileges as their counterparts in the public schools, and allowed Catholic schools a share of the Common School Fund provided by the Canadian government. What infuriated English-speaking Protestants in Upper Canada was that they did not want these schools in their section of Canada, but were forced to accept them because of the many French Canadian Catholic legislators (from the Lower Canadian section of the Assembly) determined to secure educational rights for their Catholic brothers and sisters who were a minority in Upper Canada.

The British North America Act

The sectionalism that helped to create Catholic schools also prompted Upper Canadian Protestants to demand an end to the uneasy union between Upper and Lower Canada. In 1867, the British North America (BNA) Act created Canada, with both federal and provincial governments; the latter were solely responsible for education. Catholics in the new Province of Ontario now faced a hostile Protestant majority, without the security of their old French Canadian allies from the new Province of Quebec. In advance of Confederation, with their fragile minority rights to Catholic schools in mind, Archbishop John Joseph Lynch of Toronto (1860–1888) and politician Thomas D'Arcy McGee initiated a process to secure the rights of Catholic schools. Under Section 93 of the BNA Act, all the educational rights held by religious minorities at the time of Confederation would be secured constitutionally thereafter. For Catholics in Ontario, this meant the right to establish, manage, and control their own schools, and to share proportionally in the government funds allotted to education. In time, this Section 93 would become the touchstone for most constitutional and legal debates regarding Ontario's Catholic schools.

Ryerson never thought denominational schools would survive. In the late 19th century, Catholic schools were chronically underfunded because of their small tax base, their inability to share in the business tax assessment, and their securing of only a tiny share of government school funds. Moreover, after Confederation, Ontario grew rapidly and emerged as Canada's industrial and urban heartland. The population increased dramatically and new strains were placed on the education system. Ontarians demanded progressive, high-quality education in keeping with the commercial and industrial advances of their society. Catholic schools survived the stresses of the new Ontario because of the dogged dedication of Catholic leaders to fight for legislative changes favouring their schools and because of the generosity of Catholic religious orders whose members dominated the teaching ranks in these schools, adapted to the new curricular changes, and donated much of their salaries back into the schools. Women in religious orders were notable in their ability to attain provincial teaching certification, despite the popular belief (particularly among Catholics themselves) that "nuns" would never expose themselves to the dangers of "Protestant" teachers' colleges (Normal Schools).

The Tiny Township Case

In no other instance was the self-sacrifice of Catholic school support-ers more evident than in the case of high schools. Created by an act of the Ontario Legislature in 1871, Ontario's high schools would emerge as one way in which young Ontarians could be moulded to meet the demands of their burgeoning urban industrial society. Because they had not existed as such at the time of Confederation, Catholic high schools were not eligible for provincial grants. Before Confederation, however, some Catholic schools offered instruction to older students under the auspices of the common school. Later, several Catholic schools offered "fifth book classes" (closely resembling grades 9 and 10) and were in a legal position to do so after 1899, when the government broadened its regulations regarding schools that offered a "continuation" of the cur-riculum beyond what is now grade 8. In reality, however, Catholics could direct their taxes only to public high schools and, if they so desired, could pay tuition fees to have their children receive a full high school educa-tion in "private" Catholic schools, usually run by religious orders. After decades of Catholic lobbying and sectarian fighting over this injustice, the Catholic bishops and the Ontario government agreed that a test case be brought before the courts to establish whether Catholic high schools were entitled to government funding under the terms of the BNA Act.

In 1925, Catholics in the Township of Tiny (Simcoe County) launched the poetically named legal challenge "Tiny vs. The King." By 1928, the highest court of appeal in the British Empire—the Judicial Committee of the Privy Council—offered a bittersweet decision on the Catholic high school issue: Catholics, due to the pre-Confederation precedents and the subsequent development of the "fifth book" continuation classes, had just claims to funding for grades 9 and 10; but Catholics had no constitutional right to funding beyond that, although the provincial government was at liberty to grant it, if it desired.

The disappointing result of the Tiny Township case came at a time of financial crisis and faltering morale within Ontario's Catholic schools. Since 1912, English-speaking and French-speaking Catholics had been torn apart by the Ontario government's attempt to eliminate "bilingual schools," the majority of which came under the jurisdiction of Catholic school boards. Regulation 17 restricted French-language education to grades 1 and 2, and Regulation 18 threatened to withdraw provincial funding from any boards that violated the new restrictions on French-language education in the upper grades.

Fearful of the maelstrom of linguistic and religious politics that swirled about the bilingual schools issue, the government of Premier James P. Whitney terminated its negotiations with the Ontario Catholic bishops on issues of financial relief for separate schools. The bishops were shocked that the intensity of the language issue scuttled what they thought was an imminent agreement with the government. The Catholic community was frustrated, divided, and angry; on the one side, Francophone Catholics desperately tried to preserve their distinctive schools while, on the other, their Anglophone co-religionists appeared more supportive of the Department of Education's effort to anglicize and "improve the quality of education" in the bilingual schools. In 1927, after nearly 15 years of litigation, appeals, protest, and even the suspension of the Ottawa Catholic School Board, the Ontario government relaxed Regulation 17, and limited funding for French-language education was preserved. Few at the time would have imagined that, within 60 years, Francophone children would enjoy state-supported Catholic education from junior kindergarten to grade 13. In the 1920s, however, Catholic bishops, particularly Neil McNeil of Toronto, and leading laypersons endeavoured to ease the strained relations and the lingering bitterness between English-speaking and French-speaking Catholics.

Amidst these heightened linguistic tensions and the failed appeals to the courts, it became increasingly clear that the financial pressures on Catholic schools threatened the survival of the system itself. In 1900, there were 42,397 students in the system; 25 years later, the Catholic school population had more than doubled to 95,300 students. Collectively, a low municipal tax base, a minute share of the business tax (from only those Catholic businessmen who wished to direct their taxes to separate schools), slim government grants, and a caution to keep their tax rates competitive with the affluent public school boards spelled financial hardship for Catholic schools. Facilities were old, classrooms generally were crowded, the growing ranks of lay teachers were paid less than their public school counterparts, and programs of study were limited in both breadth and variety. Despite the fact that Catholic schools matriculated students who were competitive with their peers in the public system, and although Catholic youth moved on to university in greater numbers by the 1930s, Catholic schools were still saddled with the label of "inferiority." The onset of the Great Depression in the 1930s threatened the very existence of the system.

The Catholic Taxpayers' Association

As it had done so many times in its history, the Catholic community rallied to save its schools. By the 1930s, the mantle of leadership in the fight for Catholic education was passed from the clergy to the laity. Martin J. Quinn, a Toronto businessman, organized the Catholic Taxpayers' Association (CTA) to lobby the provincial government to secure the equitable distribution of corporate and business taxes to Catholic school boards. With chapters in over 400 parishes across the province, the CTA helped to elect Mitchell Hepburn's Liberals in 1934; his government passed the much-sought legislation in 1936. The victory on the corporate tax issue, however, was short-lived. In December 1936, a wild by-election fight in East Hastings, reminiscent of the sectarian explosions of the 1850s, spelled disaster for the Liberals and convinced Premier Hepburn that the fair distribution of business taxes to Catholics would defeat his government in the next general election. The bill was withdrawn and the Catholic community's hopes for economic justice were dashed.

Canada's involvement in the Second World War (1939–1945) effectively ended the Great Depression. The post-war situation, however, merely heightened the crisis facing Catholic schools. Renewed migration from Europe, particularly from the Catholic communities of southern and central Europe, and the natural increase in population that came as a result of the "baby boom," placed increased demands on Ontario's Catholic schools. More spaces were needed for the increasing number of students in Ontario's cities, particularly in Hamilton, Ottawa, and Toronto. The suburbanization of Ontario in the 1950s necessitated new Catholic schools in formerly rural areas. A decline in religious orders and the increase in the numbers of lay teachers placed additional financial burdens on school boards that were already trying desperately to keep their school facilities and programs up to provincial standards.

Indigenous Residential Schools

The establishment of government-funded residential schools for Indigenous children pre-dated the Canadian Confederation. In a partnership between the Department of Indian Affairs and the major Christian churches, the creation of these schools appeared as a means of advancing the collective colonial agenda of conversion, assimilation, and social uplift that aimed to Europeanize and "civilize" a whole generation of Indigenous people. In the early 19th century, with the agricultural and settlement frontier expanding, Euro-Canadian colonizers no longer needed the military allegiance or environmental expertise of the Indigenous peoples living in Ontario. In fact, in the minds of the settlers, these natives appeared to be "in the way" of progress and economic development. After 1846, and the meeting between Thomas G. Anderson, Indian Superintendent for the Province of Canada, and Indigenous leaders, the government expanded its program of day schools and began building schools where Indigenous peoples could board their children. The aim of these schools was to ensure that new generations of Indigenous people would be assimilated into Euro-Canadian life, religious belief, customs, and economic culture. Enthusiastic to participate in the venture—and spread Christianity—the Christian churches of Canada eagerly became partners of the Government of the United Province of Canada, and later (after 1867), when the federal government, under the British North America Act, became responsible for Indigenous peoples.

Officially, the Ontario government distanced itself from addressing issues related to residential schools because of the federal government's jurisdiction over these schools; this position was confirmed by Mr. Justice Andrew Hope's Royal Commission in 1950, when its majority report

26

refused to address residential schools because of the jurisdictional issue. Nevertheless, while residential schools did not fall within the direct
purview of the Department of Education of Ontario, they cannot be
completely divorced from a discussion of Catholic schools in Ontario.
Many of the Catholic religious orders that built and provided the teaching
cadre for separate schools in Ontario were also engaged in the day-to-day
management of residential schools in the province. Moreover, teachers
moved with some fluidity from Ontario's separate schools to its residential
schools. Although, in the early period, religious orders such as the Oblates
and Jesuits used Indigenous languages as vehicles for teaching students,
the federal government discouraged them from doing so; these orders'
schools eventually operated in English. Catholic residential schools were
part of the assimilative program that was designed to systematically ex-
punge Indigenous languages, culture, traditions, folklore, and religion
from the Indigenous children in their care. Chronically underfunded,
these industrial schools were often cited for poor living conditions,
poor nutrition, high levels of student sickness and mortality, and, later,
child abuse by teachers and staff. The nature of the education and the
abuse of children in residential schools has recently become one of the
most controversial issues in Canadian politics and society. The story of
Indigenous Catholic residential schools, and the cultural genocide it
represented, still awaits comprehensive historical analysis, but given the
spirit engendered by Canada's Truth and Reconciliation Commission,
there may be new incentives to tell these stories.

The Hope Commission

In 1950, the offer of the Hope Commission (Ontario's first Royal
Commission on Education) to fund Catholic schools fully to the end of
grade 6, but not to subsequent grades, was indeed tempting. Such ideas
posed an interesting dilemma for Catholic leaders: an abbreviated but
equally and fully funded system at the primary–junior level, or a complete system from kindergarten to grade 13, only partially funded, and
ever-struggling at the secondary level. The Catholic commissioners, after
much deliberation with the Ontario bishops, decided to dissent from
the Commission; they submitted a brief minority report, highlighted by
historian Franklin Walker's readable and concise (less than 90 pages) out-

line of the history and constitutionality of Catholic schools. In contrast, the overdue and oversized (900 pages plus) majority report of the Hope Commission was generally ignored, as was its demand for a scaling back of government funding to separate schools. The system would survive but would continue to struggle, given the many demands placed upon it by a growing and increasingly upwardly mobile Catholic population.

Working Together towards One Goal

Given the demographic, economic, and social pressures facing the Catholic schools, Catholics once again rallied for justice. The Ontario Separate School Trustees' Association (OSSTA), the fledgling Ontario English Catholic Teachers' Association (OECTA), and the English Catholic Education Association of Ontario (ECEAO) worked hard as individual groups and, at times, co-operatively to better the situation of their schools. Co-operative lobbying efforts bore fruit in the late 1950s and early 1960s when the Ministry of Education initiated such programs as "equalized assessment," the "growth-needs factor," and the Ontario Foundation Tax Plan (1963) to "have-not" boards. Many separate school boards gleaned additional funds by means of these programs. In 1969, rural boards were amalgamated into larger county-based units with the hope that larger boards would have access to more funds, be more efficient, and provide improved programs and facilities. Together, the funding provided by the Foundation Tax Plan, and the opportunities created by board restructuring, meant a new influx of cash into Catholic elementary schools.

The Blair Commission

Catholic high schools, however, continued to suffer, because their junior grades were funded only at an elementary level, and their senior grades were sustained mainly by tuition fees. Catholics were forced to develop innovative ways to keep the high schools afloat. To make matters worse, the late 1960s and early 1970s witnessed a decline in vocations to religious life and a slow erosion through increased retirements of priests, brothers, and sisters in the schools. High schools depended on lay teachers accepting salaries that were less than the going rate, parents operating lotteries and bingos to raise funds, and students helping to clean and maintain school facilities. In the election of 1971, the Progressive Conservative party of William Davis won a healthy majority, sustained, in part, by its public refusal to extend funding to Catholic high schools. When this same government proposed changes to Ontario's tax laws that would see Catholic high school property subject to taxation, it appeared that Catholic high schools were about to sing their death song. In 1976, the Blair Commission travelled the province to assess the reaction to the tax plan: it was greeted at each stop with formidable submissions by the Catholic "partners." Through the combined efforts of clergy, trustees, teachers, parents, and students, the tax plan was scrapped and Catholic high schools dodged a bullet.

Ironically, in 1984, William Davis surprised his own caucus when he announced that there would be extended funding to grades 11, 12, and 13 in Ontario's Catholic schools. Davis regarded the decision as "justice" to Catholic schools; the cynical saw the government fishing for Catholic votes. Within three years, having faced and survived constitutional challenges, Ontario's Catholic schools finally enjoyed extended funding from junior kindergarten to the end of grade 13. Funds poured into the Catholic system, and the landscape of Ontario bore the imprint of new schools, complete with facilities, equipment, and comforts scarcely imagined in previous generations.

Bill 160

Ontario's Catholic and public education systems have witnessed an unprecedented revolution of institutional and curricular change. In 1995, school councils were created to bring parents and teachers together for the local management of their community schools. Shortly after that, the Progressive Conservative government reduced the number of school boards and cut the number of school trustees, while placing a cap on their salaries. In 1997, in a move that might have startled Egerton Ryerson himself, the provincial government suspended the right of trustees to raise taxes for schools and placed educational funding exclusively in the hands of the Province for the first time.

Thus, since the 1990s, funding for Ontario's schools is no longer a shared responsibility between the local community and the central government. For Catholics, the new financing model has meant equality of funding for Catholic and public schools. Some Catholics who have reflected upon the history of their schools have realized that finally, justice has been accorded to Catholics, under the terms of the Constitution (BNA) Act. Not all Catholics, however, have been in favour of the changes; teachers and others have seen this new centralization as jeopardizing the ability of Catholics to control and manage their own schools. There is some fear that the provincial government will take an increased role in dictating to Catholic schools, perhaps to the detriment of their distinct denominational character. In the current ideological climate, dominated by the proverbial bottom line and secular values, some people believe that the taxpayers of Ontario will be loath to support two education systems (in two official languages). In addition, the demise of publicly funded Catholic schools in Quebec and Newfoundland has contributed to a growing uneasiness about the future of Ontario's Catholic schools.

New Challenges

In the midst of adapting to the new educational landscape that resulted from the changes to boards, administrative structures, and financial arrangements in the 1990s, Catholics have grappled with the basic questions of whether their system offers a distinctive Catholic education, or simply education for Catholics and others. With money provided by the Ministry of Education for curriculum development, the Catholic partners, as coordinated by the Institute for Catholic Education (ICE), have formed three Catholic curriculum co-operatives involving representatives of all 29 Catholic school boards: one in northern Ontario, one in eastern Ontario, and one serving the central and southwestern regions of the province. These co-operatives have become hives of activity: the partners are able to sponsor conferences and workshops, produce promotional materials, and create course profiles for all grades—elementary and secondary—in which the Ontario curriculum is infused with Catholic thought and Catholic narratives. Following the benchmarks of the Ontario Catholic School Graduate Expectations, produced and promoted by ICE, the co-operatives have created distinctive course manuals that not only facilitate the delivery of the provincial curriculum, but enable teachers to firmly place a Catholic stamp on the materials they are teaching.

Similarly, these revitalized curricular initiatives have coincided with the production of distinctive Catholic course texts such as *Many Gifts*, for primary junior social studies; the *Fully Alive* series for elementary schools, on sexuality and family life; and secondary school religion texts that place a Catholic and Canadian imprint on the intermediate–senior religion curriculum. Most recently, the high school textbook *World Religions: A Canadian Catholic Perspective* has offered a serious examination of world faiths through Catholic lenses within the multicultural context of 21st-century Canada. For the first time, the great faiths of humanity are presented in dialogue with the Roman Catholic tradition.

Catholic schools in contemporary Ontario also face serious challenges relating to their student composition. One of the two stipulations of funding completion in the 1980s had been that Catholic secondary schools offer "open access" to students from the Ontario public school system. At the time, the government was making accommodation for students who might be displaced as the Catholic system expanded and local public school facilities diminished. This scenario did not come to pass, but the legacy of open access has witnessed the inclusion of many non-Catholic students in Catholic high schools. In some urban areas of the province, up to 40 per cent of a Catholic high school's population may be non-Catholic. More and more non-Catholic families are recognizing the advantages of a holistic education that nurtures body, mind, and soul: even if the religious values taught and modelled in Catholic schools differ from their own, Muslim, Hindu, Sikh, and Protestant groups acknowledge the value of having spirituality as a living part of a young person's education. For some Catholics, open access presents an opportunity for inclusion and positive Christian witness; other Catholics see this inclusion as threatening the distinctive Catholic identity of schools. In 2009, however, the Government of Ontario instituted its Equity and Inclusion Education Strategy, which mandated religious accommodation for issues of dress, diet, prayer, holy days, and religious conscience, when reasonable and without causing undue "duress" in all of the province's schools. Thus, regardless of the open access issue, Catholic schools are developing new strategies to deal with the accommodation of different religions and issues of race, gender, abilities, and sexual diversity.

Issues of the global economy have also provided challenges for Catholic education in Ontario. As the culture of North America embraces the economic doctrines of the free market and consumptive behaviour, Catholic schools have been increasingly encouraged by their constituents and by governments to enhance their revenues and local budgets by engaging in partnerships with businesses. While there are benefits to community partnerships, including relationships with local businesses, Catholic schools must reconcile their behaviour with the rich tradition of Catholic social teaching. Called by the Gospel to uphold human dignity, serve the common good, and actively pursue a preferential option for the poor, Catholic schools have had to scrutinize their business partnerships carefully. Such issues as the purchasing of the products of sweatshop labour, outsourcing labour, making decisions informed by environmental sustainability, and considering issues around just wages and benefits present challenges to the decisions that administrators, teachers, students, and parents make every day. In January 2002, in an effort to help schools make Gospel-centred decisions in these matters, the Institute for Catholic Education, with the co-operation of all its partners and the Ontario bishops, published *Guidelines for Partnerships in Catholic Education*. This document encourages schools to buy locally, observe the ethics by which products are created, and engage with businesses that show a high degree of corporate social responsibility. In some ways, these guidelines have positioned Catholic schools as a countercultural force, as they make sure that their behaviour reflects the Gospel they espouse daily in their classrooms.

One of the greatest challenges to Catholic education in the 21st century is media literacy. Within the last 20 years, innovations in communications technology have changed the way we think and behave. In Ontario, it is almost unthinkable for a school not to have access to the internet, online resources, and other wireless technologies. Some Catholic school boards have adopted a BYOD (Bring Your Own Device) policy so that students may access the latest learning technologies in the classroom and in the palm of their hands. While the iPhone and Android systems may have plugged in a record number of students and teachers to social media networks, one might question how such a revolution in communications has facilitated and enhanced personal relationships. How *social* is something like social media? With a storehouse of information ready to be unlocked, where or with whom has the process of discernment of the value of the information come? With so many acting as providers of information, have the editors and curators of information been able to keep pace? Perhaps not. Evidence of a lack of tools for weighing and evaluating information appears to abound in a society that has not come to fully understand media manipulation or acquired the fine skills of media literacy. How can students and teachers come to recognize so-called fake news when it is presented to them? Most important to Catholic schools, in an age of information overload with minimal qualitative oversight, what happened to religious ideas, theology, ethical teaching? It would appear that the comments Marshall McLuhan made in the late 1970s apply even more today than they did when he first spoke them: "How do we teach about an incarnate God in a disincarnate world?"

Now that full and equitable funding has been achieved, Catholics cannot afford to become complacent about their education system. In a secular and pluralistic society, denominational rights, particularly in the matter of schools, are not widely supported. Those who know the story of the development of Catholic schools in this province should be aware that political support for the concept of publicly funded religious education for only one denomination is slipping away. The United Nations, although it has no jurisdiction in the area, has demanded that such a discriminatory allocation of funds for education in Ontario cease. At least one of Ontario's four political parties is officially opposed to public funding for religious schools, and a second political party, in its federal wing, has a policy position that eschews public funds allocated to religious schools. Ontario's Catholics must be ever attentive to "the signs of the times" and not take for granted that Section 93 will forever protect their schools. Although it may be a very hard sell in these times, Ontario's Catholics have a responsibility to reflect upon and promote their schools as a distinctive and valuable contribution to the vitality of their faith community and to Ontario society as a whole. As history has demonstrated, and as Vatican II has confirmed, the laity have a vital role to play in the development of Catholic education. There is a need for schools that place Gospel values at the centre of a holistic education. In Ontario, the Catholic inheritance has been considerable, but so are the challenges that the future will surely bring. Such challenges have long been the companion of Ontario's Catholic schools. Perhaps contemporary leaders will learn from the stories of their predecessors and be inspired by the creativity and vision of those who shepherded the system before 1984.

Further Reading

Miller, J.R. *Shingwauk's Vision: A History of Native Residential Schools.* Toronto: University of Toronto Press, 1996.

————. "A Promise Fulfilled: Highlights in the Political History of Catholic Separate Schools in Ontario." Toronto: OCSTA, 2002.

The Royal Commission on Education in Ontario. Toronto: Baptist Johnston, 1950. Pp. 675–77.

Walker, Franklin. *Catholic Education and Politics in Upper Canada.* Toronto: The Federation of Catholic Education Associations of Ontario, 1955.

————. *Catholic Education and Politics in Ontario.* Toronto: The Federation of Catholic Education Associations of Ontario, 1964.

————. *Catholic Education and Politics in Ontario III: From the Hope Commission to the Promise of Completion.* Toronto Catholic Education Foundation of Ontario, 1986.

1

Bishop Jean-Olivier Briand
Prudence and the Art of the Possible

Library and Archives Canada (LAC), Mikan #4312602

A t first it might appear unusual to begin this series of profiles on the pioneers of Catholic education in Ontario with the story of an 18th-century cleric in New France who eventually emerged as the seventh Bishop of Quebec. However shy and mild mannered Jean-Olivier Briand appeared to his contemporaries, and perhaps wrongfully categorized as a *vendu* (someone who has sold out) by nationalist historians in French Canada, his contributions in helping to lay the foundations for Catholic liberties in Canada are unmistakable, and often overlooked.

Born near St-Eloi, in Brittany, France, on January 23, 1715, Briand studied for the priesthood with the intention of serving his home diocese. In the spring of 1741, he was recruited to assist the fledgling Church at

Quebec, France's largest North American colonial possession. Noted for his humility, quiet energy, personal poverty, and reluctance to preach, Briand eventually became Bishop Henri-Marie Pointbriand's most important assistant and was eventually appointed Vicar General of a diocese that extended from the Gulf of St. Lawrence, through the Great Lakes and Mississippi Valley, south to Louisiana and the French islands in the Caribbean.

He accompanied his bishop everywhere and was at the centre of ecclesiastical power in New France when the colony became engulfed in the Seven Years' War (1756–1763). The French forces were routed at the Plains of Abraham in September 1759, churches were destroyed by the British bombardment, and the cathedral in Quebec and the nearby episcopal palace lay in ruins. With the capture of Montreal by the British in 1760, and the signing of the Articles of Capitulation, the French regime in North America came to an end. New France was now under the control of the British Empire, ruled by a Protestant king who, according to the contemporary principle of "the religion of the Prince is the religion of the people" would likely demand that Canadian Catholics conform to the Church of England—or worse, expel New France's 70,000 inhabitants, as had been done in Acadia in 1755. This situation became most grave when Bishop Pontbriand died, making it impossible to ordain new priests to legally administer the affairs of the Catholic Church.

While the Treaty of Paris (1763), which ceded New France to Great Britain, agreed to grant "liberty of the Catholic religion … as far as the laws of Great Britain permit," realists knew that Catholicism would not enjoy freedom in the Empire, nor would British anti-Catholicism be reversed in the newly conquered territories. In this context, Briand, as Vicar General, emerged reluctantly as the temporary leader of the shattered Church. His approach to leadership could be characterized by prudence, shrewdness, gentleness, and wisdom as he began to build relationships with his new Protestant overlords as represented by Governor James Murray (1760–1766) and Sir Guy Carleton (1768–1778), who were impressed by the cleric and responded to him with much kindness and accommodation. Citing Paul's epistle to the Romans (13:1-7), Briand reaffirmed again and again the loyalty of Catholics to King George III, even going so far as having the King's name inserted into the prayer intentions during Masses throughout the diocese. Briand's relationship with

Murray evolved to the point where the Governor endorsed the decision of the Canons (priests of the Cathedral chapter) to nominate Briand as bishop, an unprecedented action that was followed by assent from the British Crown, confirmation by Rome and, eventually, in 1766, Briand's ordination in France. Six years earlier, few Catholics could have imagined a new Quebec bishop with privileges in the Protestant British Empire, and with Rome's co-operation, no less.

In 1766, Cardinal Castelli commented: "It will be necessary that the ecclesiastics and the bishop of Canada conduct themselves with all possible prudence and discretion, in order not to cause the government any jealousy in state matters." Briand became the epitome of this directive. He worked carefully and assiduously to rebuild the infrastructure of the Church, renew the priesthood, and maintain ecclesiastical autonomy from the state, while supporting the British governors politically and socially.

His co-operative spirit set the context for one of the most significant pieces of legislation influencing the practice of Catholicism in the British Empire. In 1774, as the rhetoric of rebellion was becoming more violent in the Thirteen American Colonies, Carleton influenced British parliamentarians to pass the Quebec Act, a conciliatory piece of legislation that was intended, in part, to keep Quebec loyal during a potential colonial rebellion. A noteworthy section of the Act declared: "That His Majesty's Subjects, professing the Religion of the Church of Rome and in that said Province of Quebec, may have, hold, and enjoy, the free Exercise of the Religion of the Church of Rome, subject to the King's Supremacy." While Briand was wary about what "supremacy" entailed, Carleton assured him that it was more a public statement than an expression of how the Act would work in reality. Carleton, in fact, ignored the "Instructions" that accompanied the Act, which would have placed severe limitations on Catholic autonomy and practice. For his part, when rebellion came, Briand issued a pastoral letter invoking support for the British Crown and threatening excommunication to any of his flock who threw in their lot with the Americans.

In the end, with an excellent working relationship between Carleton and Briand, the shelving of the "Instructions," and the liberal implementation of the Act, Catholics in Quebec enjoyed liberties not shared by their co-religionists almost anywhere else in the Empire—even in the neighbouring colonies of Newfoundland, Nova Scotia, and Prince Edward Island, where Catholicism was severely limited by Penal Laws imposed by the Crown. In 1774, the lands that now form much of Ontario were part of the "Old Province of Quebec"; the freedoms offered to Catholics by the Quebec Act would become precedent setting and pass into the newly created Province of Upper Canada in 1791. At that time Upper and Lower Canada would be the only Imperial possessions (outside of the Caribbean) in which Catholics could be elected to legislatures and hold a variety of public offices.

The Quebec Act became a recognition of "the collective rights" of groups in Canada, a principle that would not be forgotten when it came time to imagine how schools would be established and financed. The success of the Quebec Act owes much to Briand's embrace of St. Paul's invocation to the Romans that Christians can be true to the Gospel and still be loyal to legitimate authorities. Briand's actions were those of a Catholic leader who understood the essential values of his tradition and demonstrated prudence and moderation in his public positions while convincing potential hostile authorities of the merits of his position. As noted historian Hilda Neatby has written: "He was accused of weakness and servility, but this is rather the letter of a man clear-headed enough and humble enough not to confuse conscience with the impulses of ecclesiastical or racial pride." Briand retired in 1784 and died at the Quebec seminary on June 25, 1794. Those who treasure the enduring gift of Catholic education in Ontario owe him much.

Further Reading

Lemieux, Lucien. *Histoire du catholicisme québécois : Les XVIIIe et XIXe siècles, Tome 1, Les années difficiles* (1760-1839). Montréal : Boréal, 1989.

Neatby, Hilda. *The Quebec Act: Protest and Policy*. Canadian Historical Controversies Series. Scarborough, ON: Prentice-Hall, 1972.

Vachon, André. "Briand, Jean-Olivier." *Dictionary of Canadian Biography Online*, Vol. IV (1791–1800). http://www.biographi.ca/en/bio/briand_jean_olivier_4E.html.

2

Bishop Michael Power
Moderation and Determination

Courtesy of the Archives of the Roman Catholic Archdiocese of Toronto

J ust before sunrise on October 1, 1847, Michael Power, the first Roman Catholic bishop of Toronto, breathed his last. Citizens of this small colonial city of less than 20,000 were in shock; they had hardly known him. He had arrived in the city in June of 1842 in his newly created diocese that stretched from Oshawa in the east to Sandwich (Windsor) in the southwest, and from the shores of Lakes Ontario and Erie in the south, northward to Sault Ste. Marie and beyond to Fort William (Thunder Bay). In little more than five years Power had created parishes, begun a cathedral, created an administrative infrastructure for his diocese, built bridges between Catholics and the Protestant majority, introduced religious orders to western Ontario, and created Catholic separate schools where none had existed on a permanent basis. In 1847, however, he faced his greatest challenge: the mass migration to his diocese of nearly 38,000 refugees from the Irish potato famine. By the end of the summer, 1,124 of these newcomers, mostly Irish Catholics, had succumbed to disease, primarily typhus, or "ship's fever," as it was commonly known. By September, all of Power's priests in Toronto were stricken with it; he alone made the daily trek from his home in St. Paul's Parish to the fever sheds and emigrant hospital in the west of the city, where he comforted the sick, prayed over the dying, and waked the dead. By month's end, he too had become ill. Then he was gone, just days before his 43rd birthday.

One of the least-considered legacies of Michael Power was his dedication to the building of Catholic schools and the creative delivery of Catholic education where Catholics were too few in number to build their own schoolhouses. Some historians have suggested that his closeness to the Reverend Egerton Ryerson, the Superintendent of Schools for Canada West (Ontario), and his acceptance of Ryerson's invitation to become the chair of the province's first school board, placed Bishop Power's commitment to publicly funded Catholic education in doubt. Such arguments underestimate Power's ingenuity in delivering Catholic education to a flock that was a minority and spread thinly across the province and ignore the virtue of moderation that epitomized this young prelate's relations with politicians and non-Catholic community leaders.

Born in Halifax, Nova Scotia, in 1804, Michael Power was the eldest of William and Mary Power's eight children. Hailing from Waterford City, the elder Power was a merchant sea captain, who was more often at sea than he was at his home on Hollis Street, near Halifax Harbour. From an early age, Michael Power, influenced by local Catholic pastor and future bishop Edmund Burke, aspired to the priesthood. Due to the Penal Laws that severely restricted Catholic worship, education, and upward mobility in the British Empire (except in Quebec), Power travelled to Montreal to study at the Collège de Montréal. He was not quite 12 years old. Having completed his minor seminary education, Power entered the Seminary of Quebec and was eventually ordained in 1827, with special dispensation because of his youth. He served in the frontier missions of the St. François River Valley between Drummondville and Sherbrooke, and later in the lower Ottawa Valley at Montebello. During the rebellions of 1837–1838 he was placed under house arrest by rebels in his parish of Ste-Martine, but gained respect and notoriety when, after the failed insurrection, he intervened with the government and saved the lives of several condemned rebels in his parish. Later, at Laprairie, he caught the eye of Bishop Ignace Bourget, who made Power Vicar General of the Diocese of Montreal in 1840. One year later, Pope Gregory XVI divided the Diocese of Kingston, thereby creating a new diocese in western Upper Canada, and named Power its first bishop.

Power was overcome with the weight of these new responsibilities, knowing full well that his new diocese's 25,000 Catholics were a small and non-influential minority led by fewer than 20 priests, many of whom were reported to be lacking in discipline and fervour. Upon arrival, he wrote to colleagues in Quebec and Europe that he was truly at the "edge of civilization" and that he had "no schools, no cathedral, no seminary." Insofar as Catholic education was concerned, Power had the advantage of a new Common School Act (1841) that made provisions for religious minorities to establish a separate school, where numbers warranted. This acknowledgement of the collective rights of religious minorities (Catholics in what is now Ontario; Protestants in Quebec) was the fruit of the labours of Power's predecessor, the late Bishop Alexander Macdonell of Kingston, who had lobbied the British Colonial Office and used his strong political connections to win piecemeal concessions for Catholic education in the 1830s. Power came to understand that in Canada West (Ontario), Catholic schools, although guaranteed some financial support from the government, were difficult to establish and even more difficult to staff and maintain. It became clear to him that in addition to taking advantage of separate school provisions, which were confirmed in law in 1843 and 1846, the thinly stretched Catholic population would have to be creative in delivering a *holistic* education across the diocese.

In 1845 he advised Father Michael Mills of St. Thomas: "The Catholic children should be allowed to remain in a separate room until the usual lessons from the Holy Scriptures shall have been read; they can read themselves a chapter from the authorized Catholic version of the New Testament. It would be preferable in every way if parents of Catholic children could have a separate school of their own; but this must depend in great measure on the number of Catholics in each locality." As alter-

41

natives to forming their own separate school boards, because of a thin population base, Power encouraged his priests to have their parishioners hold catechism classes in the church after Sunday Mass, or arrange for religious instruction in the local common school at the end of a teaching day. Wherever possible, and where numbers of Catholics might be the majority in certain districts like Essex County or northern Simcoe County, the bishop urged Catholics to become active in the Common School Board, hire a Catholic teacher, and essentially exert influence over the curriculum in that public school.

By far his most lasting legacy in Catholic education was his recruitment of members of the Society of Jesus (Jesuits) to his diocese in 1843 to work among Indigenous peoples and, in 1847, his successful invitation to the Institute of the Blessed Virgin Mary at Rathfarnam, Ireland, to send its Loretto Sisters to Toronto to establish both private tuition-based schools and regular separate schools under the current legislation. In so doing, Power laid the groundwork for the engagement of male and female religious orders in the enterprise of Catholic education in the western portion of Ontario. From their humble first establishments in Sandwich (Windsor) and Toronto, these religious orders would build a network of Catholic schools across the province, and with the arrival of dozens of new orders over the next 20 years, men and women religious would come to dominate the administration and the teaching corps of separate Catholic schools for generations.

The question remains: If Power was so dedicated to many ways of delivering Catholic education, why did he become involved in public schools? Power knew that as leader of the Catholic minority in the province, it was critical to cultivate excellent relations with Protestant leaders and be a voice of moderation in an environment where sectarian tension was never far from the surface. He became good friends with Toronto's Anglican Bishop, John Strachan, who in 1846 recommended to Ryerson that he appoint Power to the new governing board responsible for curriculum, teacher training, and supervision of all of Canada West's schools. Board members were so impressed by Power's grace, intellect, and moderation that they elected him chair. Power knew well that his position would help him stay close to the centre of power in the education system, a position that would make it much easier for him to defend Catholic education. When he died, not only did Ontario lose an educational pioneer, but Ryerson admitted he had lost a great friend. For its part, the Catholic community lost a model of leadership, a broker of peace, an ingenious steward of Catholic education, and the founder of at least 10 new separate schools. Given the manner of his death, it was not surprising that contemporary observers also claimed that the Church had witnessed a "martyr to charity." In 2017, Cardinal Thomas Collins announced that the Archdiocese of Toronto would initiate a process to beatify the city's first bishop, a pioneer of Catholic education in western Ontario.

Further Reading

McGowan, Mark G. *Michael Power: The Struggle to Build the Catholic Church on the Canadian Frontier*. Montreal & Kingston: McGill-Queen's University Press, 2005.

———. "What Did Michael Power Really Want? Questions Regarding the Origins of Catholic Schools in Canada West." CCHA *Historical Studies* 68 (2002): 85–114.

Nicolson, Murray W. "Michael Power, the First Bishop of Toronto, 1842–1847." CCHA *Historical Studies*, 54 (1987): 27–38.

3

Mother Teresa Dease, IBVM
Gentle Fortitude

From the Author's Collection

orn in Naas, County Kildare, Ireland, on May 4, 1820, Ellen Dease was the youngest of five children born to Oliver Dease, an officer and surgeon in the British Navy, and Anne Nugent, a scion of one of Ireland's most prominent Catholic aristocratic families. Her father, brothers, and nephews were well integrated into the imperial military complex, travelling the world and representing a tiny Catholic minority who had been accepted into the officer class of the British military. Orphaned at an early age—her parents had died within a week of one another—Ellen was sent to be raised by her grandmother. Gifted in languages, Ellen studied in France, but decided to return to Ireland. In 1845, she joined a new religious order, the Institute of the Blessed Virgin Mary

(IBVM, or Loretto Sisters), who had founded a house at Rathfarnum, outside of Dublin, in 1822. Internationally, the IBVM was by no means a new religious community. Mary Ward (1585–1645), an English recusant Catholic (one who retained her Catholicism despite persecution from the established Church of England), had founded the Institute in 1609; its houses spread from continental Europe to India, Mauritius, Gibraltar, and quietly to York, England, in 1686, amidst the tumult of Protestant–Catholic sectarianism. Ellen was given the religious name Teresa and prepared herself for a life of teaching.

In 1847, however, during the worst year of the Great Irish Famine, Bishop Michael Power of Toronto visited the Abbey at Rathfarnum with the hope of recruiting some Loretto Sisters to his frontier diocese to lay the foundations for a network of Catholic schools. Considering that his diocese encompassed what is now all of the province of Ontario from Oshawa in the east to Fort William (now Thunder Bay) in the west, such a mission would promise to be the most formidable challenge yet faced by the Irish sisters. In the summer of 1847, the Institute's superior, Mother Teresa Ball, agreed to Bishop Power's request and sent four sisters and a novice to found a mission in Canada. Mother Teresa Dease was among these recruits who included two biological sisters, Ignatia and Valentina Hutchison (the former of whom would serve as superior of the Toronto house), Gertrude Fleming, and Bonaventure Phelan. The group left Rathfarnum on August 5 and boarded a sailing ship at Cobh (Queenston); it took six weeks to cross the Atlantic en route to New York. Dressed in civilian clothing, so as not to raise undue attention to themselves, the "Ladies of Loretto" proceeded by steamer up the Hudson River to Albany, and then took a train to Rochester, where they boarded a boat for Toronto.

They arrived in Toronto on September 16, 1847, joining hundreds of other Irish immigrants who had ventured to Toronto via Quebec, fleeing the famine conditions in their homeland. The city was in the midst of a typhus epidemic which had claimed the lives of hundreds of migrants and many citizens of Toronto. No one met them dockside, so they ventured to the episcopal palace by cab. In her diaries, Teresa Dease recalled that Bishop Power was ashen when he greeted them at the door; his two resident priests were stricken with typhus (little did he know that he was incubating the infection as well), and he became anxious that these women would contract the disease themselves. He found them lodgings with a local Catholic convert and philanthropist, Samuel Lynn; before long, the sisters were establishing schools in the city. Power had wanted both a "free" separate school and an academy for the training of young Catholic women.

Teresa Dease's first years in Toronto were calamitous, yet despite the adversity she faced, she emerged as a model of deep piety and gentle fortitude. Within two weeks of her arrival, Bishop Power died of typhus, leaving the Loretto Sisters without their patron. The diocese would be without a bishop for two and a half years, during which time Dease's community would be decimated. Sister Bonaventure Phelan would die in April 1849, and Sister Gertrude Fleming would pass away on Christmas Day, 1850. Fleming's story, Dease recounts, was tragic. Fleming, who was one year younger than Dease, was asked to teach at a new Catholic school in the west of the City of Toronto, a considerable distance from the "mother house," located in the east end. The Institute in Ireland had been semi-cloistered and taught pupils on the premises of their convent, but in Canada, the conditions that confronted Dease and her sisters necessitated that they move about the city. This was less than ideal, given the mush of Toronto's unpaved streets: snow in winter and mud the rest of the year. In her travels, Fleming contracted tuberculosis in her bones, and was forced to have one leg amputated when the growth on her knee proved too painful for her to bear. She was fitted with a prosthesis and was determined to keep teaching, but gangrene set in and Fleming died. Less than three months later, in March 1851, Mother Ignatia died, and her younger sister returned to Rathfarnum. In less than three years, only Dease remained of the original pioneers. At the age of 31, Mother Teresa Dease became the superior of the Lorettos in North America, a position she would hold for 38 years.

Despite her own fragile health, Dease built the foundations for her Institute and for Catholic education generally throughout the province. Her leadership was marked by a gentleness, propriety, and gentility that betrayed the courage, fortitude, and creativity that became hallmarks of the Loretto Sisters. At her request, the Irish mother house at Rathfarnum continued to send new recruits to Toronto; locally, Dease successfully recruited young Canadian women, including Charlotte Lynn, daughter of the Lorettos' first lay patron, and great-granddaughter of a former Anglican Bishop of Carlisle. Lynn was given the religious name Ignatia, an obvious act of homage to the first Canadian superior.

With her growing band of sisters and their impressive reputation for excellence in teaching, Dease embarked on an expansion of Catholic schools across the province. The Lorettos founded several separate schools in Toronto, and in 1853 built new separate schools in Brantford and London. Three years later, the Lorettos were in Guelph, where they laid the foundations of a school beside the cathedral-esque Church of Our Lady, which dominates the city's skyline. In 1857, Dease was asked to establish a Catholic school in Belleville, the first of several ventures in that city. Four years later, the Lorettos founded a school in Niagara Falls, which sat adjacent to the falls and became Dease's favourite place among all the Loretto establishments. In 1865, the Lorettos undertook an academy in Hamilton, which was followed by further establishments in Lindsay, Stratford, and finally Joliette, Illinois. From humble beginnings in Toronto, the Loretto network now encompassed two countries and six dioceses, anchored by 13 religious houses.

Most important, the Loretto Sisters became representative of how the survival of Catholic schools rested on the living endowment of women and men in religious life. Like other religious orders that would come after them, the Lorettos built schools, donated their salaries back to the schools, developed curriculum, ran huge educational establishments, and conformed with the highest standards of professionalism, as mandated by the Department of Education. Without the work of the sisters, brothers, and clergy in these formative years, Catholic education in Ontario would have died the slow death from financial starvation that Chief Superintendent Egerton Ryerson had predicted and hoped for.

After she had been nearly four decades at the helm of the Institute, Mother Teresa Dease's health began to fail. She died on July 1, 1889, in Toronto, but her remains were transferred by a funeral train to her beloved Niagara, where she was laid to rest. Although her own humility would eschew any such self-description, she was one of the great pioneers and shepherds of Ontario's Catholic schools.

Special note of thanks to Elizabeth Smyth, "Mother Teresa Dease and the Loretto Foundations in Canada," a paper presented at the Catholic Sisters as Global Missionaries conference, University of Notre Dame, Notre Dame, Indiana, April 6-8, 2017.

Further Reading

Costello, Bride, IBVM. *Life and Letters of Rev. Mother Teresa Dease.* Toronto: McClelland, Goodchild and Stewart, 1916.

Lei, Christine. "Material Culture at the Loretto School for Girls, Hamilton, 1861–1971." CCHA *Historical Studies* 68 (2000): 92–113.

Norman, Marion, IBVM. "Making a Path by Walking: Loretto Pioneers Facing the Challenges of Catholic Education on the North American Frontier." CCHA *Historical Studies* 65 (1999): 92–106.

4

Bishop Armand-François-Marie de Charbonnel
Tireless Advocate

When he arrived as the newly appointed Bishop of Toronto in the autumn of 1850, Armand de Charbonnel found the diocese in disarray. Almost three years had elapsed since the death of the founding bishop, Michael Power, and the institutional structures that this "martyr to charity" had founded were withering on the vine. Charbonnel's diocese was still one of the largest on the planet, encompassing all of the territory in what is now Ontario, between Oshawa and Windsor, extending over the Great Lakes as far as Fort William (now Thunder Bay). The Catholic population had increased by 60 per cent since the time of

49

Bishop Power to over 80,000; part of the increase was due to the migration of refugees from the Irish famine, from 1846 to 1850. Charbonnel had only 33 priests to serve this growing Catholic population, stretched thinly across his vast diocese. Moreover, the Protestant majority (400,000 persons) in Canada West (Ontario's official name from 1841 to 1867) had become increasingly hostile to the Catholic minority because of what non-Catholics perceived as papal aggression under Pope Pius IX in Europe and from what was seen as French Catholic domination of the Legislative Assembly of the Province of Canada, whose elected members served the united provinces of Canada East (now Quebec) and Canada West (now Ontario). Charbonnel's primary concern was to rebuild the Church infrastructure, one of the primary components of which was a fledgling Separate Catholic School System.

Born in Château du Flachat, France, in 1802, Charbonnel was the second son of a French count and ardent royalist during the French Revolution. Early in life, the young Charbonnel steered clear of a political career and turned to the Church, where he had established himself as a scholar at Montbrison, Annonay, and the Seminary of St. Sulpice in Paris. He was ordained in 1825 and became a priest of the Society of St. Sulpice (Sulpician) the following year. He worked as a professor of theology and scripture at the Seminary of Lyons; some historians say that Charbonnel decided to be a missionary in North America to avoid being appointed either superior of a seminary or bishop of a French diocese. He worked with fellow Sulpicians in Montreal in the 1830s and attempted to learn English in Baltimore. In 1845, he preached the priests' retreat in Toronto at the invitation of Michael Power. Here he made a lasting impression, and when no successor to the late bishop could be found, local priests requested that Charbonnel be considered. Much to his regret, he was consecrated bishop by Pius IX in Rome on May 26, 1850.

Charbonnel's brief tenure as bishop was marked by tremendous energy. He finished building St. Michael's Cathedral, recruited priests and seminarians (which resulted in nearly twice the number of clergy by the time of his departure in 1860), regularized church finances, established charitable institutions (including the St. Vincent de Paul Society), founded the Toronto Savings Bank (1854), and imposed an ultramontane spirituality (an adherent of a Catholic revival focused on the ultimate authority of the Pope) on his diocese, including the revival of Catholic devotional practices, sacred music, and religious art. He himself donated the floral window above the high altar in St. Michael's Cathedral.

His most important project was the building of Catholic schools both as centres of a holistic education that situated Catholic teaching at its heart, and as a protection from what he feared was Protestant proselytizing in the province's common schools. At a time when sectarian bitterness was rising in the province, Charbonnel insisted that Catholics be given greater liberty in founding separate schools in the towns and cities of Canada West and that legislative restrictions upon Catholics to establish, manage, and control financing to their schools be repealed. Charbonnel was alarmed by an incident in Georgetown in 1851, in which Catholic students in the common school (there was no separate school) were subjected to Protestant scriptures and hymns, which was a contravention of legislation in 1850 protecting Catholic students by allowing them to leave class for such periods. As he himself recounts, "After many representations, I was obliged to enter into an open war against our system of schools; my adversary ... is afraid and tries to scare me ... [We] will do all that we have done and more to oppose the cruel persecution that devours our children here ...." Charbonnel's adversary was none other than Egerton Ryerson, Canada West's Superintendent of Schools. Preferring that there be a generic Christianity embedded in public schools, which all citizens might share, Ryerson opposed the extension and strengthening of Catholic education and resisted Charbonnel's demands. Their war of words was passionate, bitter, and public, with their letters published for popular consumption.

Charbonnel must be credited with adopting and expanding upon the blueprint already laid out by Michael Power. The new bishop sought the assistance of a religious order he had known in France, calling them to the diocese to help him build schools and charitable institutions for his burgeoning Irish flock. In 1851, the Congregation of the Sisters of St. Joseph answered the call, via their house in Philadelphia, and sent sisters who would eventually lay the foundations for schools, hospitals, and social services across the diocese. That same year, his colleague in the Brothers of the Christian Schools (De La Salle) accepted his call and immediately made plans to establish a school for boys. In 1852, Charbonnel called upon his old teachers from Annonay, the Congregation of St. Basil (Basilians), to found a seminary and college. These Basilian priests eventually consolidated the Christian Brothers' school with their own and established St. Michael's College. In inviting these religious orders to the province, Charbonnel had set in motion the creation of a broad network of separate schools run by members of religious orders who would build schools, staff them, create curriculum, and donate their salaries back to the schools. Ryerson, who had never anticipated or hoped for a long life for Catholic schools, seriously underestimated Charbonnel's "secret weapon" of the men and women of consecrated life who would sustain separate schools for the next century.

On the legislative front, Charbonnel and his supporters won several significant victories that would prove to be a lasting legacy for Catholic education in the province. In 1853, The Supplementary School Act, section IV, guaranteed Catholics the right to elect their own trustees, build schoolhouses, hire teachers, raise school taxes, and claim a "fair share" of the Common School grant—while being exempted from paying the Common School Tax. Noting, however, that the implementation of the Act was uneven across the province, Charbonnel and his Episcopal colleagues, Patrick Phelan of Kingston and Joseph-Eugène Guigues of Ottawa, rallied Catholic politicians to correct the injustices. In May 1855, the Legislature began an acrimonious debate on a Separate School Bill proposed by Legislative Councillor Étienne Taché. When it passed on the strength of French Canadian Catholic votes from Canada East, the Taché Act made clear that only five ratepayers were required to found a Catholic school, and this could be done regardless of the denominational affiliation of the local common school teacher. The Act provided for trustees of separate schools to control and manage their schools and collect taxes. These principles were reinforced in subsequent legislation and were eventually protected within Section 93 of the Canadian Constitution (The British North America Act, 1867).

Charbonnel had proven to be a tireless advocate for Catholic education both by securing legislative rights and by improving teaching, curriculum, and leadership of Catholic schools. On other fronts, he had less success; he often quarrelled with his priests and laypersons, who felt he didn't really understand or appreciate the Irish. These disputes were complicated further by the fact that he never managed to master the English language. On two occasions he requested to Rome that he be relieved of his episcopal duties. In 1860, Rome accepted his resignation and he returned to France. He became titular Bishop of Sozopolis and served as auxiliary Bishop of Lyon. In 1891, having retreated to a life of contemplation, prayer, and study in a Capuchin friary, Charbonnel died. His short and turbulent life in Ontario was marked by the creation of two new dioceses in Hamilton and London (originally Sandwich) in 1856, and by the remarkable growth and stability of the province's separate schools.

Further Reading

Careless, J.M.S. *Brown of the Globe:* Vol. 1. *The Voice of Upper Canada, 1818–1859.* Toronto: MacMillan, 1959.

Nicolson, Murray. "Bishop Charbonnel: The Beggar Bishop and the Origins of Catholic Social Action." CCHA *Historical Studies* 52 (1985): 51–66.

Walker, Franklin. *Catholic Education and Politics in Upper Canada.* Toronto: The Federation of Catholic Education Associations of Ontario, 1955.

5

Sister Bernard Dinan, CSJ
Patience and Perseverance

Courtesy of the Sisters of St. Joseph of Toronto Archives

On October 7, 1851, four women arrived in Toronto at the request of the new bishop, Armand de Charbonnel. Entrusted with establishing an orphanage, these members of the Congregation of the Sisters of St. Joseph (CSJ)—Delphine (Maire-Antoinette Fontbonne) [Superior], Alphonsus (Sarah Margerum), Mary Martha (Marie Bunning), and Bernard (Ellen Dinan)—were the Canadian vanguard of a religious order originally founded in France in 1650, suppressed during the French Revolution, resurrected in 1807, and recently called to North America, first at St. Louis, in 1836, and later at Philadelphia. In a very short time, however, this foursome would put in place the foundations of what would become the largest order of women religious in Ontario. The legacy of the Sisters of St. Joseph would be felt profoundly in Ontario's health care system, social services, and publicly funded Catholic schools.

By 1856, Sister Bernard Dinan, the youngest of the pioneers, was the only remaining member of the original foundation left in Toronto. Sisters Delphine and Alphonsus had died and Sister Mary Martha was busy establishing the CSJs and their work in Hamilton and its newly created diocese. Sister Bernard was born Ellen Dinan in 1829, daughter of Thomas Dinan and Ann Sullivan, at Macroom, County Cork, Ireland. Her family migrated to the United States either prior to or during the Great Irish Famine; in 1849, she entered the Congregation at her adopted city of Philadelphia. In March 1852, Ellen made her final profession of vows in St. Michael's Cathedral and was immediately appointed head of novices, a position that she held for four years. Part of this time was spent in Sandwich (now Windsor), where she founded a CSJ-sponsored institution that served as hospice, house for the poor, and Catholic school. The multi-talented Sister Bernard appeared able to manage all three operations. By 1858, she was appointed as superior of a similar operation in Niagara, which was then part of the Diocese of Toronto. It was on the Niagara peninsula that she served in a variety of administrative roles, including Superior of the CSJs in St. Catharines.

In 1869, Sister Bernard became Superior-General of the entire Congregation, which was now operating schools, health-care facilities, and social services in the Dioceses of Toronto, London, and Hamilton. Under her leadership, Toronto's House of Providence received a new wing (1873), new schools were built under the provisions of the Scott Act, and private boarding schools for "respectable young girls" were opened, most notably Notre Dame Academy in Toronto. At the request of Toronto Bishop, later Archbishop, John Joseph Lynch, she began a school for women who had been interned in the provincial "Lunatic Asylum" on Queen Street. In addition, she oversaw the building of a new academy in St. Catharines, the CSJ takeover of the St. Nicholas Home for Working Boys; the building of the Notre Dame des Anges boarding house for working women (forerunner of St. Michael's Hospital); and the enlargement of the CSJ mother house near Clover Hill, in Toronto. As the network of CSJ-managed schools expanded, Sister Bernard was also responsible for allocating teachers to each facility from among the new recruits to the Congregation.

Even while in administration, however, Sister Bernard never let go of her love of teaching. She could often be found among the young women of CSJ schools on field trips or taking a personal interest in the quality of education and the residential conditions of the schools in her care. She was modelling what had always been a fact within the Congregation: regardless of the task you had been given, particularly teaching, you were expected to serve the poor and sick wherever they were found. By 1873, Sister Bernard's little band of four had grown into a religious order of 131 sisters in Toronto alone (the London and Hamilton jurisdictions had become independent of Toronto in 1868 and 1856, respectively): the sisters managed a network of schools and services that stretched from Oshawa to Windsor, and from Barrie to Niagara Falls.

Sister Bernard's life took a sharp and unwelcome turn in 1874 when Archbishop Lynch removed her as Superior-General because of an incident between a resident student and an unnamed sister at St. Joseph's Academy. The student became a *cause célèbre* in the public press as a victim of "papal tyranny," even though the adolescent testified in an affidavit that she had borne false witness against the Academy. Lynch had Sister Bernard reassigned to Oshawa, in an effort to distance the Congregation and Archdiocese from the alleged scandal and begin leadership anew. Sister Bernard, a model of patience and grace, continued the grassroots work in education and social services that had made her a much-loved leader in the Congregation. By 1882, she had moved again, to the St. Catharines convent school, and five years later was teaching in Thorold. Her work was cut short within the year when she was recalled to Toronto to manage the expansion of the Sacred Heart Orphanage at Sunnyside, an institution that both housed homeless children and provided a Catholic curriculum for the residents within an extraordinary "home-like" pedagogical setting. By 1891, the new bishop, John Walsh, opened a centre for 300 youth which included dormitories, playrooms, classrooms, workshops, a refectory, and a chapel.

Sister Bernard celebrated her golden jubilee as a sister at Sunnyside in 1900, and died in her sleep there one year later on September 20, 1901.

In 50 years, she had witnessed her Congregation become the undisputed leader in Catholic education with elementary schools and academies in the dioceses of Toronto, London, Hamilton, Peterborough, Pembroke, and Sault Ste. Marie (which included North Bay and the current city of Thunder Bay). Her patient leadership provided wise oversight to the building of a Catholic school system of which 21st-century Ontario Catholics are fortunate beneficiaries.

Further Reading

Bouchard, Mary Alban, CSJ. "Pioneers Forever: The Sisters of St. Joseph of Toronto and Their Ventures in Social Welfare and Health Care." In Mark G. McGowan and Brian P. Clarke, eds. *Catholics at the Gathering Place: Historical Essays on the Archdiocese of Toronto, 1841–1991.* Toronto: Canadian Catholic Historical Association, 1993. Pp. 105–18.

Smyth, Elizabeth. "Christian Perfection and Service to Neighbours: The Congregation of the Sisters of St. Joseph, Toronto, 1851–1920." In Elizabeth Gillan Muir and Marilyn Fardig Whiteley, eds. *Changing Roles of Women within the Christian Church in Canada.* Toronto: University of Toronto Press, 1995. Pp. 38–54.

Young, Mary Bernita, CSJ. *Silent Growth: The Life and Times of Sister Bernard Dinan.* Toronto: Sister of St. Joseph Historical Publications, 1986.

6

Sir Richard William Scott
One Who Thirsted for Justice

Persons with even the slightest knowledge of the history of Catholic education in Ontario are usually able to recall that the Scott Act of 1863 was one of the cornerstones of Catholic rights to their state-supported denominational schools. Few, however, might be able to offer the simplest detail of the life of Richard Scott, who may well have been one of the most colourful Catholic politicians in Canadian history. This teetotalling, vegetarian, compulsively physically fit father of 10 had his finger on the pulse of most of the major political events of the nation until his death on April 23, 1913, at the age of 88.

Richard William Scott was born in Prescott, Upper Canada, on February 24, 1825, the son of Irish immigrants. His father, Dr. William James Scott, had been born in England but served with the British army in his family's native County Clare. The Scotts were prominent in Irish politics, with one of Dr. James's nephews serving as financial agent for Daniel O'Connell, "The Great Liberator." It was said that at the age of 13, young "Dick" Scott watched the battle of Windmill Point unfold as the local militia, led by his uncle, drove back the "patriot" rebels to the United States. With activism and political pedigree etched into his DNA, Scott excelled in school and was admitted to the bar of Canada West in 1848; four years later, at the age of 27, he was elected mayor of Ottawa. In 1851 he married a popular Irish singer, Mary Heron, who had been performing in Ottawa, and together they had 10 children (three boys and five girls were living; a girl and a boy had died as infants).

In 1857, Scott was elected to the Legislative Assembly of the Province of Canada, representing constituents in Ottawa and briefly supporting the ministry of Liberal-Conservative leader John A. Macdonald. Shortly after his election, in 1858, Scott was able to openly advocate for the selection of Ottawa as the permanent capital of the United Canadas. He would become better known, perhaps notorious in some circles, for his repeated attempts to better the situation of Canada West's (now Ontario's) Catholic separate schools. Denominational schools for both Catholics and Protestants had been made possible by legislation as early as 1841. At that time, the Day Act made it permissible for ratepayers to form a separate school where numbers warranted. In Canada East (now Quebec), Protestants exercised this right, fearing the omnipresence of the Catholic Church over that section of Canada's schools. Similarly, in Canada West, the tiny Catholic minority set up separate schools as protection from Protestant dominance in most sections of the province. In reality, Protestants also set up separate schools in Canada West, fearing the dominance of any one denomination—Anglican, Methodist, or Presbyterian—over local public or common schools. In the 1840s and 1850s, the rights of Catholics to control and manage their schools became more clearly defined; by 1855, five Catholic ratepayers could establish a separate school, staff it, lay claim to government revenues from the

Common School Fund, and refrain from directing their property taxes to the local public school.

For Scott, this was certainly not enough. He had noted that Catholics in rural areas were handicapped by distance and numbers and were generally incapable of forming separate schools. He also noted that government revenues were not distributed equally between the common and separate schools. In 1860, he read his first bill into the assembly with an intent to correct the problems in the financing and management of Catholic separate schools. George Brown's "Clear Grit" Party (the forerunner of today's Liberal Party) opposed the extension of any support for separate schools. The Grit preference, and that of their official mouthpiece the Toronto *Globe*, was one public school system for all, with no special privileges to any religious group. The bill failed in the House, as did a second bill in 1861, and a third died on the order paper when the house adjourned in 1862.

Scott, if anything, was persistent. In 1863, he managed to weave together an alliance of Les Bleus (Catholic French-speaking members of the house from Canada East), moderate Liberals, and Liberal-Conservatives (Macdonald's minority party from Canada West). Together, this alliance of the sectional parties pushed Scott's bill through the House, much to the anger of Brown and his Grits, who declared that this type of coercion by French Canadian Catholics was no longer tolerable and the Constitution would have to be changed. Ironically, Brown's declaration led to the negotiation of a new federation, and separate school rights became, in one sense, the godmother of a new Canadian Confederation.

Many in the House considered the Scott Act to be the final piece of legislation pertaining to separate schools. The Act confirmed the right of five Catholic ratepayers to establish a separate school board, call a public meeting of Catholics, and elect three trustees, who would manage the affairs of the board and raise school taxes from the declared ratepayers. It also provided for such a school to be instituted in rural areas, instructing that a three-mile limit from the schoolhouse be the geographic zone from which ratepayers could be solicited and students could be drawn. The Act provided for the union of small school boards into larger units if necessary, and for an equitable sharing of any government grants by public and separate schools. The amount received would be based on the number of students attending the Catholic school (Section 18). Separate school supporters would not be required to pay the common school rate. For their part, however, Catholic schools agreed to submit to the Council of Public Instruction with regards to school inspection, curriculum materials, and teacher training. In 1867, when denominational school rights were enshrined in Section 93 of the British North America Act as they existed "by law," the Scott Act provided the benchmarks for the legal establishment of separate Catholic schools in Ontario.

Although he was not a Conservative and had in fact supported more moderate Liberals, Scott's alliance with Macdonald cost him at the polls, and in 1863 he was defeated. He returned to politics when he was elected to the new Legislative Assembly of Ontario in 1867, where he served as Minister of Crown Lands for Premier Edward Blake in 1871. In 1874, he accepted Prime Minister Alexander Mackenzie's invitation to enter the Canadian Senate, where he served until his death. In Mackenzie's Liberal government, Scott served as Secretary of State. In this capacity he ensured that Catholic schools would be included in the provision of the Northwest Territories Act (1875), which would allow for their continued existence when the provinces of Alberta and Saskatchewan were created in 1905. It was also during this ministry that Scott achieved fame for a second Scott Act, and perhaps one better known to historians outside of Ontario. In 1878, Scott successfully introduced a bill (The Canada Temperance Act) that would allow for municipalities to exercise a "local option" and prohibit the sale of alcoholic beverages. Scott himself was a lifelong abstainer and believed that alcoholism was at the root of much criminal behaviour.

Scott's voice could be heard on numerous issues, whether it was on the necessity of laying more telegraph cables linking Europe and Canada; effecting compromises to ensure Manitoba Catholics could retain religion classes after school hours in public schools; standing up to British generals during the Boer War, asserting the supremacy of the Canadian Parliament on the Canadian contribution; or breaking ranks with many English-speaking Catholics in Ontario by supporting and advocating for French-language school rights in the province. His was a reasoned and courageous voice, thirsting for justice. At the time of his death in

April 1913, his great legacy to Catholic schools was 50 years in his past. Regarding this monumental legislation, Cardinal Manning, Archbishop of Westminster, wrote to Scott: "We owe you our hearty thanks, for the example of the Dominion has more weight in the mother country than any other part of the Empire … May God strengthen you in defending Catholic education." Interestingly, this example was passed on through his children and descendants. His great-grandson, Ian Scott, was Ontario's Attorney General who, in the 1980s, guided the legislation for funding completion to Catholic high schools through the constitutional challenges in the courts.

Further Reading

Clarke, Brian P. "Sir Richard William Scott." *Dictionary of Canadian Biography*, XIV (1911–1920). Toronto: University of Toronto Press, 1998. Pp. 913–16. http://www.biographi.ca/en/bio/scott_richard_william_14E.html.

Scott, W.L. "Sir Richard Scott, 1825–1913." CCHA, *Reports* 4 (1936): 46–71.

Walker, Franklin. *Catholic Education and Politics in Upper Canada.* Toronto: The Federation of Catholic Education Associations of Ontario, 1955.

7

Thomas D'Arcy McGee
Eloquent Advocate

Library and Archives Canada (LAC), C-15369

On the night of April 7, 1868, Thomas D'Arcy McGee, member of Parliament from Montreal and perhaps one of the most gifted orators in the British Empire, left a late sitting of the House of Commons in Ottawa and made his way back to his apartment, two blocks away on Sparks Street. As he was opening his outer door, he was approached by a stranger who aimed his revolver at McGee's head and fired, killing him instantly. It was the first of very few political assassinations in Canadian history—one that claimed one of the most eloquent advocates of Catholic schools this country has ever known.

Born in 1825 in Carlingford, County Louth, Ireland, McGee was one of eight children born to James McGee and Dorcas Morgan. James McGee was a civil servant in the Irish Customs and Revenue department; the family moved to Wexford, where Thomas was raised and educated. It was here that he developed his love of learning, Irish history, poetry, and culture, which he soon translated into a life's work of publishing. In 1842, he relocated to the United States, where he wrote and edited for the Catholic newspaper the *Boston Pilot*, mostly on themes denouncing British rule in Ireland and raising support for the repeal of the political union between Britain and Ireland. In 1845, he returned to Ireland to become a parliamentary correspondent for Daniel O'Connell's *Freeman's Journal*. As his anti-British positions hardened, McGee left O'Connell's Repeal Association and became prominent in *Young Ireland*, a radical political movement that sought an Irish cultural revival as an integral part of Ireland's desired autonomy from Britain. After a failed rebellion and a brief arrest in 1848, the radical McGee returned to America, where he used his own newspapers in New York, Boston, and Buffalo to advance the cause of Irish freedom.

The anti-Catholicism evident in the United States in the 1850s, however, prompted a conversion in McGee's ideas. Ironically, he became attracted to Canada, where the British, through the precedents set by the Quebec Act of 1774, accorded Catholics greater freedom and respect than he witnessed in Ireland or the United States. Writing from New York in 1856, McGee stated that, "disappointed in this country [USA] of that religious freedom that was the hope of so many emigrants, I have resolved to make my future home and that of my children, in the valley of the Ottawa." In 1857, at the encouragement of the local Irish Catholic community, McGee and his family settled in Montreal: McGee established *The New Era* newspaper and was elected to the Canadian Legislative Assembly by Christmas that same year.

McGee was first aligned with the "Reform" government of George Brown and A.A. Dorion of the French Canadian "Rouges." This appeared to be an odd alliance, given McGee's re-embracing of the Catholic Church and Brown's fierce opposition to separate schools. It would appear that "liberal politics" was the gel that held their partnership together—but not for long. Although McGee supported the idea of mixed religious schools on the Irish model, with separate schools as a possible fallback position, he soon incurred the wrath of the Catholic bishops on one side, and, on the other, found his political allies uncompromising in their opposition to denominational schools, as they feared that common schools would be placed at risk. By 1862, McGee had another conversion when he recognized that the Conservative Party, headed by an alliance of John A. Macdonald and George-Étienne Cartier of the French Canadian "Bleus," was the only political force willing to defend Catholic school rights. Much to George Brown's disgust, and that of the Toronto *Globe*, McGee eloquently defended the Separate School Bill proposed by fellow member of Parliament Richard Scott. Although not authorized to do so by either the bishops or Catholic school supporters, McGee went so far as to declare in the House that the Scott Bill was the "final" piece of legislation needed to secure Catholic school rights in the Upper Province. In 1863, the Scott Act became law—and the foundation for publicly funded Catholic schools in Ontario.

Macdonald appointed McGee Minister of Agriculture in the "Great Coalition" government that steered the way to Confederation. During the negotiations for the union of Britain's North American colonies, McGee became a key player in ensuring that the denominational rights of minorities to retain separate schools would be protected under the terms of Confederation. When it became clear that the newly designated provinces would have primary jurisdiction over education, the Protestant minority in Lower Canada (Canada East/Quebec) and the Catholic minority in Upper Canada (Canada West/Ontario) feared that their educational privileges would be taken away by the hostile majorities in each province. McGee became instrumental in having the British North America Act contain clauses ensuring that if denominational schools, as they existed in law, were threatened, they would be protected through the intervention of the federal government. The resultant Section 93 has become the constitutional assurance that the rights of religious minorities, as regards their schools, are sacrosanct.

McGee's Irish politics never seemed to have left him, although his radicalism did. He became outspoken about the idea that Ireland should have the type of constitutional self-government that was enjoyed by Canada and that the Irish republican radicals of the Fenian Brotherhood should be opposed at all costs. In 1865, his famous "Wexford Speech," in which he denounced the Fenians on their home turf, may have signed his death warrant as a "traitor to the Irish cause." It is highly likely that Patrick Whelan, the man accused of, convicted of, and hanged for McGee's murder, had strong Fenian ties. While McGee's political life changed direction several times, his devotion to the Church remained strong. Today, his pew at St. Patrick's Church, Montreal, is marked by a memorial commemorating one of Canada's great orators, writers, and visionaries.

Further Reading

Dooley, Ann. "D'Arcy McGee, Fenianism, and the Separate School System in Ontario." In Robert O'Driscoll and Lorna Reynolds, eds. *The Untold Story: The Irish in Canada*, Vol. 1. Toronto: Celtic Arts of Canada, 1988. Pp. 501–20.

Wilson, David. *Thomas D'Arcy McGee*. Vol 1: *Passion, Reason, and Politics, 1825–1857*. Montreal & Kingston: McGill-Queen's University Press, 2008.

———. *Thomas D'Arcy McGee*. Vol. 2: *The Extreme Moderate, 1857–1868*. Montreal & Kingston: McGill-Queen's University Press, 2011.

8

Archbishop John Joseph Lynch
Diplomacy, Advocacy, and Controversy

Courtesy of the Archives of the Roman Catholic Archdiocese of Toronto

Not surprisingly, there is some dispute about the birthplace of the controversial John Joseph Lynch, the third bishop and first archbishop of Toronto. While often considered a native of County Monaghan, Ireland, Lynch was in fact born in 1816 in the parish of Clones, in a small section in County Fermanagh, now Northern Ireland. Given that his father was a schoolteacher, it was not unexpected that the young Lynch pursued his formal education with vigour and made Catholic schools a priority during his priestly life.

He was educated in Lucan (County Dublin) and Paris, where he became a member of the Vincentian Order of missionary priests. Ordained in 1843, he was eventually sent to the mission field in Texas, where he remained only from 1846 to 1848. Having contracted malaria, he was moved to Vincentian institutions in Missouri and New York. It was in Niagara that he founded Our Lady of the Angels Seminary (now Niagara University, Lewiston) and caught the eye of Toronto bishop Armand de Charbonnel. After preaching a mission in Toronto in 1858, Lynch was nominated by Charbonnel to be his coadjutor with right of succession. When the latter resigned the See, the former Irish missionary and teacher became bishop of Toronto in 1860, inheriting a territory that stretched from the Niagara peninsula to Georgian Bay. When Pope Pius IX elevated Lynch to the rank of Archbishop in 1870, his provincial territory included all of Ontario west of the Diocese of Ottawa. His influence across Ontario was as enormous as his Metropolitan See, a fact recognized by the leading politicians of the day: Conservative Prime Minister Sir John A. Macdonald in Ottawa and Liberal Premier Oliver Mowat in Toronto, who sought his support.

As bishop responsible for the growth of Catholic education, Lynch became known as a builder. Early in his episcopate, he agreed with Catholic politician Richard Scott that the Taché Act, which provided separate schools with the rights of self-management, did not go far enough. Lynch became a strong supporter of Scott's subsequent bill in 1863, which gave separate schools greater access to public funds and extended their establishment into rural areas. When, in 1867, separate schools would be at the mercy of provincial governments, Lynch argued for a strengthening of the provisions of the Scott Act and supported formal protection for denominational schools under the BNA Act. Lynch also fostered the creation of additional Catholic separate schools in the cities of central Ontario and supported the founding of educational institutes by religious orders of men and women. He assisted the Soeurs de Notre Dame in their foundation of the Notre Dame Institute for Women, a hostel that Catholic women often used when studying for careers in teaching at the Toronto Normal School. In 1860, when Lynch was ordained bishop, there were 14,708 students in 115 separate schools across the province. By the time of his death in 1888, close to 260 separate schools were educating

34,571 students. Much of this success in numbers was due to Lynch's tireless advocacy and behind-the-scenes diplomacy.

In a partnership with long-time Liberal Premier Oliver Mowat (1872–1896), Lynch secured numerous concessions for separate schools. Some of the advantages gleaned by Lynch's quiet diplomacy were that Catholic ratepayers could declare themselves separate school supporters only once, instead of having to do so every year. Lynch also managed to win Mowat's approval for appointing special Catholic inspectors for separate schools. When secondary schools were created in 1871, the same rights to high schools were not extended to the separate system, although Lynch won concessions that a separate school trustee be elected to public school boards to protect Catholic interests in the high schools. The most important reforms, however, came in 1886, when upon Lynch's lobbying, Catholic tenants could now declare separate school support and Catholic businesses could voluntarily direct their business taxes to local Catholic school boards.

His diplomatic efforts met with resistance from both Protestants and Catholics. Protestant pundits and politicians denounced the so-called Lynch–Mowat Concordat and described Mowat, a Presbyterian, as being a mere pawn of the minions of Rome. Mowat knew full well that at election time, Catholics would be more favourable to his Liberal party in key swing ridings, and that working with the leading bishop was a political necessity. On the other side, Lynch's suffragan bishops (those who represent dioceses within an ecclesiastical province headed by an archbishop) complained that he was not loud enough in his public proclamations for Catholic school rights; Lynch knew better and preferred the private letter and quiet meetings over blustering from the pulpit. He recognized that the Catholic population of Ontario was in a fragile position, still at the mercy of the overwhelming Protestant majority.

Moreover, Lynch knew enough of controversy without having to create more. When he asked, in 1882, that the anti-Catholic poem *Marmion* by Sir Walter Scott be removed from the senior examinations in secondary schools, the press howled that this was tantamount to papal interference in Ontario's public schools. When Mowat and the Minister of Education, Adam Crooks, refused to bow to public pressure to retain the poem, it became an election issue in 1883. The Liberals, with Lynch's quiet help, easily took 50 of 80 seats, and the *Marmion* issue was laid to rest. More fury erupted from the press, Conservatives, and Orangemen when it was discovered that the new Minister of Education, George Ross, had asked Lynch to review a book of scripture passages intended for use in Ontario's public high schools, in an effort to make certain nothing would be offensive to Catholic students in these institutions. There were more howls of indignation over Catholic censorship of what became derided as "the Ross Bible" in 1884. But it was much ado about nothing; Lynch had only recommended that "who art" replace "which art" in the Lord's Prayer, and that its last line (which is not normally recited by Catholics) be omitted. Never far away from either scholarly arguments with local Protestant clergy or as a witness to violent clashes between Catholics and Protestants in his city and in the province generally, Lynch, in 1875, argued for patience on the part of Catholic Christians: "We tolerate what we cannot help, we endure what we cannot cure."

Not all of his Catholic flock thought highly of his leadership on the schools issues. He clashed repeatedly with a group of Toronto Catholic school trustees over their overt Irish nationalism and what he considered their scandalous "anti-clericalism." For their part, a bloc of trustees led by Remigius Elmsley accused the archbishop of excessive meddling in board affairs, protested temporal aspects of his superintendence of schools, and accused him of mishandling Church properties designated for schools. Above all, they objected to the fact that elections to the board were held by open vote and not a secret ballot, which enabled Lynch to use "pressure" to have as many of his allies, including several priests, elected to the board annually. "I disapprove of secret balloting," argued Lynch. "It is a great, great incongruity that a free man should hide a vote." It was only after his death that a bill proposed in 1894 by James Conmee, a Catholic member of provincial Parliament for Nipissing, allowed separate schools to employ the ballot.

When Lynch died in 1888, he left an impressive legacy in Catholic education as a skilled negotiator, a calm advocate, and a magnet for controversy. His detractors often overlooked his deep spirituality, his devotion to Our Lady of Knock, and his strong belief in the power of prayer. His last request was that he not be buried in the crypt of St. Michael's

Cathedral, which was his right; instead, his remains should rest under the Cathedral's north wall, where passers-by could see his resting place and say a prayer for the repose of his soul.

Further Reading

Humphries, Charles W. "Archbishop John Joseph Lynch." *Dictionary of Canadian Biography*, Vol. XI (1881–1890). http://www.biographi.ca/en/bio/lynch_john_joseph_11E.html.

McKeown, H.C. *The Life and Labors of the Most Rev. John Joseph Lynch*. Toronto and Montreal: James A. Sadlier, 1886.

Stortz, Gerald J. "Archbishop John Joseph Lynch of Toronto: Twenty-eight Years of Commitment." CCHA *Study Sessions* 49 (1982): 5–23.

9

James Francis White
Devotion to Duty

From the Author's Collection

When he died in Toronto at the age of 64 in May 1922, the Toronto *Globe* eulogized James White as a great "instructor" and scholar who was noted for his "devotion to duty" in his service not only to Catholic education, but to teacher training programs in the province generally. "He was beloved and admired by all who knew him," reported the *Globe*, "as a courteous Christian gentleman." Despite his many contributions to the improvement of separate schools in Ontario, he is virtually unremembered by the Catholic community, and no school has been named in his honour.

James Francis White was born in Trenton, Canada West, on November 18, 1857, one of three children born to shoemaker James White and Ellen Mahoney. James Francis and his two sisters all became educators, with one sister joining the Loretto Sisters. James Francis attended local elementary and secondary schools, graduating from the Toronto Normal School at the age of 17, winning its prestigious Dufferin Medal. Holding a First Class Certificate, he taught for six years and eventually was appointed principal of separate schools in Lindsay and Belleville. Active in the development of Catholic teachers across the province, the highly articulate White served as General Secretary of the Convention of Separate School Teachers, which held its inaugural meeting in Hamilton in 1878.

His dedication to teaching and to the improvement of educational standards caught the eye of Premier Oliver Mowat, who appointed him the first Inspector of Separate Schools for the Province of Ontario. Prior to this, Catholic schools had been inspected by non-Catholics from the Department of Education, which had raised objections from Catholic leaders, particularly Archbishop John Joseph Lynch of Toronto. Due, in part, to the friendly relations between the Archbishop and the Premier, sometimes known derisively as the "Lynch–Mowat Concordat", the appointment of White was intended to further enhance the Catholic management of the 193 separate schools in Ontario.

White travelled from Windsor to the Ottawa Valley and as far north as Mattawa to ensure that Catholic schools maintained as high a standard as public schools. If his early annual reports are any indication, White was not pleased by much of what he witnessed during his inspections. Unafraid of any backlash from ratepayers, bishops, clergy, or heads of religious orders, White was highly critical of the poor textbooks, lack of English-language education (in French and German regions), substandard school facilities, inadequate teacher training, and lackadaisical attitudes towards school attendance. For White, getting Catholic students to school at the appropriate age in the First Form (grades 1 and 2) and keeping them until age 14 (as mandated by the government) would ensure that Catholic children could meet life's challenges with the appropriate training.

White's criticism of the low standards in many Catholic schools did not endear him to certain bishops. When he criticized the use of too many different series of textbooks in some schools, and the poor quality and outdated approaches in Catholic readers, several bishops were horrified by the Inspector's "disrespect" of Catholic education. White, however, won concessions from more sympathetic bishops and educators that the superior public school readers might be used; his advocacy for better texts proved to be a catalyst for the creation of Copp Clark's *Canadian Catholic Reader* series, published in 1899. The textbooks, with their handsome design, contained a collection of Canadian-themed stories combined with religious poetry, Bible stories, and lives of prominent saints.

Perhaps one of the fiercest battles in the early history of Catholic education was prompted in 1893 by James White's criticism of the lack of provincial teacher qualifications among instructors in separate schools. In his report of 1892, White severely reprimanded Catholic trustees for changing teacher placements too often, for lacking a coherent and uniform system of grading practices, and for accepting substandard student achievement. These problems pointed to a lack of the proper certification of Catholic teachers, most of whom were members of religious orders and few of whom held Ontario First Class Certificates. Many religious had acquired some training within their congregations, or if from Quebec, had trained under different standards from those of Ontario. When Anglophone ratepayers and trustees in Ottawa objected to Francophone trustees hiring the Brothers of the Christian Schools (De La Salle), a controversy erupted within the Catholic community over the teacher qualification issue. Non-Catholics joined the fray, claiming that the Catholics were now confirming what was always known about many separate schools—the teachers did not meet provincial standards. Based on White's findings, a Legislative Commission had already confirmed the poor standing of the Christian Brothers in Ottawa, and the order withdrew from the city.

When the Brothers attempted a return to Ottawa in 1904, at the invitation of Francophone trustees, the battle over qualifications was presented to the courts. J.D. Grattan, an Anglophone Catholic ratepayer and teacher in Ottawa, sued the city's Catholic school board for attempting to hire unqualified teachers. The bishops and Catholic leaders were horrified by the case. They maintained that Catholics had a constitutional right to these teachers; religious orders had their own training programs; and women religious would never subject themselves to the "Protestant" environment of the Normal Schools—they would simply return *en masse* to Quebec or the United States. It would be the end of Catholic education. Justice Hugh Ryan, himself a Catholic, ruled in Grattan's favour, claiming that only teachers who taught in the system prior to 1867 had an exemption from formal provincial qualifications, under Section 93 of the British North America Act. The decision was upheld despite an appeal made to the Judicial Committee of the Privy Council, the highest appellate court in the British Empire.

In 1907, White (no longer Inspector) intervened privately with the Premier, James P. Whitney, the Minister of Education, R.A. Pyne, and the Superintendent of Education, John Seath, to provide legislation that would ease Catholic religious, both men and women, into appropriate levels of certification. Based on years of teaching experience and a few short summer courses, separate school teachers were given a reasonably clean and easy path to their First, Second, or Third Class certificates under the Seath Act (1907), "An Act Respecting the Qualifications of Certain Teachers." Above all, White reported to the Premier that "I am sure that at least nine tenths of Catholics of the province wish to have only qualified and capable teachers placed in charge of their schools." Despite all of the dire predictions, the religious orders quickly certified their members under the new provisions, there was no exodus from Ontario, and the separate schools were made stronger.

White had retired as an inspector in 1902, and took up the post of principal of the Ottawa Normal School, a position he held for 20 years, until his death. There he practised what he preached: he taught teacher candidates English, the history of education, and school management. Despite White's earlier clashes with some bishops, Archbishop Neil McNeil of Toronto recognized his abilities, faithfulness to the Church, and devotion to Catholic education when in 1912 he named White a member of an educational advisory committee to the Ontario bishops.

Further Reading

Canadian Catholic Readers, Book 4. Toronto: Copp Clark, 1899.

Choquette, Robert. *Language and Religion: A History of French–English Conflict in Ontario.* Ottawa: University of Ottawa Press, 1975.

Power, Michael. "James Francis White." *Dictionary of Canadian Biography* Vol. XV (1921–1930). http://www.biographi.ca/en/bio/white_james_francis_15E.html.

10

Bishop Michael Francis Fallon, OMI
Controversial Crusader

From the Author's Collection

Born the eldest of seven sons to Dominic and Bridget Fallon in Kingston, Ontario, on May 17, 1867, Michael Francis Fallon would become a towering figure in the Canadian Church. He was educated by the Christian Brothers before entering Kingston Collegiate Institute; he graduated from high school in 1883 and then briefly attended Queen's University before switching to the University of Ottawa, an Oblate institution which was named a pontifical university by Pope Leo XIII. Fallon was the complete all-round student, majoring in humanities, active in the English debating society, founding editor of *The Owl* newspaper, and a passionate rugby player. He graduated *cum laude* in 1889 with a BA in English; that same year he entered the diocesan seminary, but after three years of study elected to join his mentors in the Oblates of Mary Immaculate (OMI). The Oblates sent him to Europe for study; after a brief sojourn in the Netherlands, he entered the Gregorian University in Rome and graduated with a Doctor of Divinity degree in 1894.

Given his passion for Catholic education and his fervent belief that Catholics of his home province should not only be well educated in Catholic schools but should pursue post-secondary degrees to advance in Canadian society, it is not surprising that he was appointed to teach at his alma mater, the University of Ottawa, in 1896. Not only did he hold the chair of English Literature, but also, true to the combination of education and masculinity in Catholic schools of the day, Fallon coached the university's rugby team, which was undefeated for two years. His life at the university not only revealed his scholarly bent and his assertive personality as a coach, it witnessed his emergence as an advocate for English-language Catholic education from elementary to post-secondary. His time at the university was cut short because he became embroiled in a power struggle between French- and English-speaking Oblates for control of the University of Ottawa and its contested bilingual nature. Fallon envisioned the institution as Anglophone and run by Irish and Irish Canadian priests. The OMI superiors had other ideas; they restored Francophone leadership and appointed Fallon, the vice-rector, as the new pastor of St. Joseph's Parish—across the street from the university. From the nearby pulpit, Fallon was passionate in his defence of English-speaking Catholic rights, and he continued his public advocacy for the British Empire and Irish Home Rule. Despite his popularity among parishioners, the local Oblates had had enough of him. In 1901, he was transferred to the Oblate-run Catholic parish in Buffalo, New York.

Fallon's exile would last eight years, during which time he continued to preach and write. He even took out American citizenship, figuring that his views on language and culture would forever keep him away from Canada. He was wrong. In 1909, the See of London became vacant when the bishop, Fergus Patrick McEvay, was moved to Toronto to become its sixth bishop and fourth archbishop. Because of the strong presence of Franco-Ontarian Catholics in Windsor, Essex, Kent, and Lambton, the new bishop needed to be fluently bilingual. As a result, there was considerable power-playing afoot between the Anglophone and Francophone bishops and priests to secure their own candidates for the vacancy. In the end, the Apostolic Delegate, Donatus Sbarretti, came to believe that the expansion of the Catholic Church in Canada rested in those clergy and lay Catholics who spoke the English language. Much to the horror of French Canadian priests and Bishops, who remembered Fallon from his Ottawa years, Pope Pius X appointed the bilingual Fallon as the fifth bishop of London, a position he held until his death in 1931.

Fallon's passion for a separate school system that produced excellence in its students was shaken as he encountered numerous bilingual schools in his diocese. Although the official language to be used for instruction in Ontario schools had been mandated as English as early as 1885, French- and German-language instruction persisted well into the 20th century. In January 1910, the French Canadian Education Association of Ontario (ACFEO) held a congress in Ottawa which advocated for the extension of French-language rights through both public and separate school systems in Ontario. Fallon and other Anglophone bishops became alarmed at these demands. In bilingual schools, the language of instruction was primarily French, and Fallon observed that this did a grave disservice to Franco-Ontarian children because it hampered their prospects for employment and advancement in Ontario. When meeting with Provincial Secretary W.J. Hanna in May 1910, Fallon wanted it made known to Minister of Education Dr. R.A. Pyne that he was resolved to eliminate bilingual separate schools in his diocese. The contents of Fallon's secret meeting were leaked to the press by a Franco-Ontarian civil servant working in the Public Works department. The French-language press and clerical and lay leaders voiced their protest of Fallon's remarks, and he faced near rebellion from several Francophone priests in his own diocese.

That same year, Fallon's episcopal colleagues had been negotiating with the government of Conservative Premier James P. Whitney for financial and textbook concessions for separate schools. As the language tensions escalated over bilingual schools, most of which were Catholic, the Whitney government suspended negotiations with the bishops. The Church in Ontario was now publicly split along linguistic lines, with French Canadians publicly denouncing Fallon and suggesting that he and his fellow Irish clergy were merely "les orangistes" (Orangemen) in disguise. The government commissioned inspector F.W. Merchant to inspect the bilingual schools; his report, issued in 1912, offered a balanced view of the schools, praising the qualities of some schools while offering strong criticism of those that appeared to have lived up to Fallon's expectations. The government, now feeling the pressure from its Orange caucus members, overreacted and implemented Regulation 17, which effectively prohibited all French-language instruction after grade 2. While Fallon had nothing to do with the legislation, he was tarred with the same anti-French brush as the government.

By 1914, efforts by the Vatican to move Fallon back to the United States failed; he steadfastly refused to leave unfinished what he had begun. Seven years later, Rome ruled in Fallon's favour, dismissing charges made against him by a consortium of his French Canadian priests. In the interim, when parishioners rebelled at Our Lady of the Lake Parish in Ford City, a suburb of Windsor, and refused to allow Fallon's newly selected priest to enter the parish rectory, the police were summoned and a riot ensued. When thousands of parishioners refused to back down, local authorities read the Riot Act and the protest was suppressed by the army. The linguistic fight over separate schools in Fallon's diocese had become yet another lightning rod for French–English hostility, in the midst of Canada already being torn asunder by the conscription crisis during the Great War.

In fairness to Fallon, his primary concern was the extension of effective Catholic education; his own efforts in the Diocese of London provide sound evidence for this. During his tenure as bishop, the population of his diocese increased from about 60,000 to over 100,000. Separate school students in the diocese doubled to 14,000 as Fallon directed the expansion of the separate schools across the rural and urban areas of the diocese. He was instrumental in founding St. Peter's Seminary in London in 1912, which eventually provided a local alternative to St. Augustine's Seminary in Toronto, which had national aspirations. Fallon also helped to establish the affiliation between his St. Peter's School of Philosophy (a division of the seminary) and the non-denominational University of Western Ontario. Similarly, he was instrumental in the affiliation of Brescia College, run by the Ursuline Sisters, with that university and its move from Chatham to the Western campus in London. Fallon also worked out a similar affiliation arrangement between Assumption College in Windsor and Western.

Perhaps his finest hour for Catholic education came in 1922, when he spearheaded the movement to extend public funding to Catholic secondary schools, something that the Ontario government had denied since the creation of the high school system in 1871. On February 11, 1922, sponsored by the Catholic Women's League, he gave a three-hour oration to a packed Massey Hall in Toronto, demanding "constitutional rights" not "sectarian privileges" for Catholic schools in Ontario. He took "mudslinging" journalists to task for their misreading of the historical facts about Catholic schools. Arguing for more equitable funding, Fallon claimed that Quebec had treated its Protestant minority fairly and "placed the educational world on a footing of equality before the law. That was the intent of the Fathers of Confederation—nothing less would have been accepted by the Protestant minority of Quebec and no less would have been accepted by the Roman Catholic minority of Ontario." His passion helped to launch the legal challenge made by Tiny Township for educational grants to be extended to Catholic high schools.

Complications arising from diabetes took Fallon's life in 1931. He had left plenty of controversy in his wake: his support for conscription in 1917, his enthusiastic efforts to recruit soldiers and chaplains for the Canadian Expeditionary Force during the Great War, his advocacy for Irish self-government resembling the Canadian model; and his advancement of rights for English-speaking Catholics in Ontario. What is often overlooked was his ceaseless dedication to preserving and extending publicly funded Catholic schools in his native province.

Further Reading

Barber, Marilyn. "The Ontario Bilingual Schools Issue, 1910–1916." *Canadian Historical Review* 47 (September 1966): 227–48.

Choquette, Robert. *Language and Religion: A History of French–English Conflict in Ontario*. Ottawa: University of Ottawa Press, 1975.

Fiorino, Pasquale. "The Nomination of Bishop Fallon as Bishop of London." CCHA *Historical Studies* 62 (1996): 33–46.

11

Napoléon-Antoine Belcourt
Language Guardian of the Faith

Sénateur Napoléon-Antoine Belcourt (1860-1932), Ottawa, [ca 1900]. Université d'Ottawa, CRCCF, Fonds Association canadienne-française de l'Ontario (C2).

One of his contemporaries referred to him as the head of the "movement to liberate Franco-Ontarians." In 1924, none other than the arch–French Canadian nationalist priest Lionel Groulx awarded him the "grand prix" of the *L'Action Française* movement on the Feast of Adam Dollard Des Ormeaux, the 17th-century hero who allegedly "saved" New France from annihilation. The symbolism was not lost on the throngs of Montrealers who witnessed the ceremony. In 1971, an Ottawa high school was renamed in his honour. Yet, in our own time, few Ontario Catholics outside the Franco-Ontarian community will recognize the name Napoléon Belcourt or his intrepid fight to preserve Catholic schools in the French language.

Napoléon Belcourt was born of French Canadian parents in Toronto on September 15, 1860. He returned to his family's home province to be educated at St. Joseph's Seminary in Trois-Rivières, and later Université Laval in Quebec City, where he graduated with a master's degree in law in 1882. That same year he was called to the bar in Quebec, but in 1884 decided to apply to the bar in Ontario and practise in Ottawa. He taught law at the University of Ottawa in 1891 and four years later received his doctorate in law from that same institution, all the while serving as a Crown Attorney for Carleton County. After the execution of Métis leader Louis Riel in 1885, he stood firmly opposed to the Conservative Party of Sir John A. Macdonald, whom he blamed for Riel's death, and joined the Liberals. In 1896, he was elected to the federal Parliament for the constituency of Ottawa, whose citizens re-elected him in 1900 and 1904. From 1904 to 1906 Belcourt served as speaker of the House of Commons, until Prime Minister Wilfrid Laurier appointed him to the Senate, where he served from 1907 until his death in 1932. Belcourt's political background and networks would serve him well as he embarked upon the greatest political fight of his career: the cause of French-language Catholic schools—bilingual schools—in Ontario.

The French Canadian Catholic population had grown exponentially in Ontario in the late 19th and early 20th centuries. By 1911, they constituted roughly 10 per cent of the provincial population and just under half of the Catholic population. Franco-Ontarian Catholics were conspicuous in their rural settlements in eastern Ontario, in the lumbering, railway and mining communities of northern Ontario—which they dubbed *Nouvel Ontario*, and in the Anglo-Protestant heartlands of Simcoe County and in the Essex-Windsor region. By law, French Canadian Catholics had controlled both public and separate schools in these districts, where the language of instruction was primarily French. There was unease among the Anglo-Protestant population about the growing presence of the French language and culture in Ontario, and rumblings even from the Catholic bishop of London, Michael Francis Fallon, that these bilingual schools were entirely French in nature and were most inefficient. Sensing the threat to faith-based education in the French language, Senator Belcourt and others founded the French Canadian Education Association of Ontario (ACFEO) to advocate for not only the retention, but also the expansion of French-language education in the province. Citing his belief that Confederation was a pact between the two founding peoples—Anglophone and Francophone—Belcourt led the charge for the recognition of French Canadian education rights, and therein the right to found and nurture faith-based schools in the French language. Language would be the guardian of the faith. As the first president of ACFEO, Belcourt mobilized his Liberal connections, held rallies (which included support from Laurier himself), and lobbied the provincial government.

In February 1912, after a two-year investigation of bilingual schools, school inspector Dr. F.W. Merchant reported to James Whitney's Conservative government that these schools employed poorly qualified teachers who offered an inferior level of education, particularly in the English language, which by necessity students would need to find employment in the rapidly industrializing Ontario of the early 20th century. While not necessarily intending to do so, Merchant's report played into the hands of the Anglo-Protestant majority in Ontario, whose Francophobia and anti-Catholicism were inflamed by the alarmists and rhetoricians in the Loyal Orange Lodge. Conservative politicians and pundits applied pressure on the Whitney government to eliminate French-language schools once and for all. In June 1912, the government introduced Regulation 17, which prohibited the use of French as the language of instruction beyond grade 2. Shortly thereafter, the government approved Regulation 18, which threatened to deprive provincial funding from any school board that disobeyed Regulation 17. Belcourt was now in the midst of a titanic struggle to save French-language schools, most of which were Catholic.

His Anglo-Celtic co-religionists were of little help. All the Anglophone bishops acquiesced to Regulation 17 and, particularly in the case of Bishop Fallon, openly supported the legislation in the name of improving the quality of education. Fallon was a lightning rod of controversy who had become, in the eyes of Belcourt and others, essentially an "orangiste" (Orangeman) in a soutane. In fairness to the bishops, however, they had spent much time before 1910 negotiating with the Whitney government for tax relief, distinctive textbooks, and better funding for Catholic separate schools, a lengthy process in which they had made considerable headway. When ACFEO was formed, the government panicked, ceased negotiations with the bishops, and instead moved to thwart Belcourt and his colleagues. What resulted was a dark chapter in the history of Ontario's Catholics, as the Church split along linguistic lines with what appeared to be, at least in Belcourt's eyes, an unholy marriage of the Orange and the Green pitted against his side.

With his legal expertise, Belcourt led ACFEO's court challenges against Regulation 17 and against the Ontario government when it imposed a commission to run the Ottawa Catholic School Board when the board refused to comply with Regulation 17. By 1919, however, Belcourt recognized that the ACFEO defence had failed and that the tactics of open resistance to the government were futile. The courts of appeal had upheld the regulation, the Catholic bishops demanded respect for the law, and the Vatican had issued two letters to Canadian Catholics demanding peace between linguistic factions. Belcourt understood that his tactics must change for the faith and culture of French Canadians to survive west of the Ottawa River.

In 1920 he regained the presidency of ACFEO and began a two-pronged strategy. First, he would gather sympathetic Anglophones to argue for the survival of the French Canadian fact, as implied by the Confederation agreement. To this end he inspired the founding of the Unity League, which courted over 150 notable Anglophones to support the cause of national unity and the rights of French Canadian Catholics. He also secured the friendship of the multilingual Archbishop of Toronto, Neil McNeil, who himself was anxious to heal the rift in the Church and promote national unity. For Belcourt, however, bridging the two solitudes was not enough. A second dimension of his plan was to address the old Merchant Report head on: if French Catholic schools could prove themselves to be sound in curriculum and pedagogy, there would be no reason to impose any restrictive legislation on them. Inspired by Belcourt, French Canadians set up private schools in places like Green Valley (north of Cornwall) or within the beleaguered Ottawa Separate School Board, introduced more recent pedagogical techniques, hired excellent teachers, and developed a solid curriculum. Belcourt caught the attention of Premier G. Howard Ferguson, himself an Orangeman from Kemptville and a former supporter of Regulation 17, who now softened his position and allowed for Belcourt's plan to unfold. French Catholic schools in Green Valley and Pembroke displayed the best of what a bilingual school could offer.

While inspectors complained of the unevenness of the education in bilingual schools despite the reforms, the Ferguson government decided that each school would be judged on its own merit, thereby preserving the reputation of the entire bilingual school system. In 1927, Belcourt's tactics proved victorious when Ferguson declared a relaxation of Regulation 17. The two-pronged strategy of building alliances and demonstrating curricular excellence had paid off, and French-language Catholic schools lived to fight another day. Ferguson even accepted the teacher training programs provided by the University of Ottawa for French Catholic teachers.

With these victories in hand, Belcourt retreated from public life and continued his legal advising of the Ottawa Separate School Board while serving as president of Connaught Park Raceways, thereby satisfying his passion for horse racing. His later years were not peaceful. His detractors, mostly Anglophone Conservatives who used the pages of the *Ottawa Journal* as their pulpit, accused him of taking more money than his due when working as legal counsel for the school board. They also harangued him on his "divorce" from his second wife, surely a scandal in his day. (His first wife died in 1901; he had remarried in 1914.) In spite of the scandalmongers, Belcourt was exonerated by the courts. He died at his summer home in 1932, having remained faithful to his Senatorial duties until his health failed him. His ability to save French Catholic schools provided a foundation for the system of French Catholic schools, which today extend from junior kindergarten to grade 12. Napoléon Belcourt deserves to be remembered as the emancipator of French-language Catholic education in Ontario.

Further Reading

Choquette, Robert. *La Foi : Gardienne de la Langue en Ontario, 1900-1950.* Montréal : Bellarmin, 1987.

————. *Language and Religion: A History of French–English Conflict in Ontario.* Ottawa: University of Ottawa Press, 1975.

Zucchi, John., ed. *The View from Rome: Archbishop Stagni's 1915 Reports on the Ontario Bilingual Schools Question.* Montreal & Kingston: McGill-Queen's University Press, 2002.

12

Father John Joseph O'Gorman
Priest, Educator, and Padre

From the Author's Collection

One of the many overlooked pioneers of modern Catholic education is the dynamic and controversial eastern Ontario priest John J. O'Gorman. He was born in Ottawa on March 8, 1884, the son of John O'Gorman, a civil servant, and Elizabeth Rose Warnock. A lifelong supporter of and advocate for Catholic schools, O'Gorman was educated at St. Patrick's School and later attended the University of Ottawa, where he earned BA and BPhil degrees. Intending to enter the priesthood, he studied in Germany, Belgium, and Rome before returning to Canada for his priestly formation in the Grand Séminaire in Montreal. On December 21, 1908, Archbishop Joseph Duhamel ordained O'Gorman in his home parish of St. Patrick's in Centretown. He served briefly at St.

Brigid's Parish in Lower Town before going to Rome, where he earned a doctorate in canon law. As a scholar he was widely read and spoke eight languages: English, French, Spanish, Latin, Greek, Italian, German, and Irish. Upon his return to Canada he was sent to St. Philip's Parish in Richmond, Ontario, but in 1913 was transferred as founding pastor of the new Blessed Sacrament Parish in Ottawa's Glebe neighbourhood. There he would remain for the rest of his priestly life, building the parish's social, liturgical, and educational foundations.

As an advocate for Catholic separate schools in the English language, he became a thorn in the side for leaders of Ottawa's French Catholic community. He consistently challenged the linguistic imbalance in Ottawa Catholic schools, a situation that witnessed to what he deemed to be the French domination of the separate school board at the expense of the Anglophone minority. As a result, he did not support the existence of bilingual schools, which he believed offered an inferior education to Francophone children. During the bitter struggle over these schools, the young O'Gorman battled with *Le Droit*, the local French daily newspaper, which attacked him as "anti-French." Given these heated exchanges with Franco-Ontarian educational leaders over the Ottawa Separate School Board's violation of Regulation 17's prohibition on bilingual (more or less French-language) education after grade 2, Archbishop Charles Hugh Gauthier forbade Dr. O'Gorman and his nemesis, Father S. Hudon of Rockland, from addressing "religio-racial questions" in the press.

When the Great War erupted in August 1914, O'Gorman emerged as an ardent supporter of the Canadian and Imperial war effort. From his pulpit and in the press, O'Gorman was able to weave Irish Canadian Catholic participation into a narrative that acknowledged that when the Empire had called, dating back to the Boer War, Canada's Irish Catholics had answered robustly. In January 1916, he took a break from his pastoral and school duties and received Archbishop Gauthier's blessing to join the Canadian Chaplain Service. Later that year, while serving with the 3rd Brigade, O'Gorman was struck by shrapnel when hauling the Canadian dead from no man's land. Demobilized back to Ottawa to convalesce, O'Gorman was not idle: he helped to overhaul the Canadian Chaplain Service and became the inspirational leader of Catholic Army Huts, a program to provide Canadian troops with chapel and recreational facilities. He did a second tour of duty, receiving the Order of the British Empire for his exemplary service as a military chaplain. In 1919 he returned to Ottawa and re-engaged in his passion—the strengthening of Ontario's Catholic schools.

O'Gorman's return to Blessed Sacrament was by no means retiring. He leaped into the challenges of a growing parish by building schools, erecting a new church building, contributing to local social service agencies, researching and writing about Ireland and its culture (including a plan to be the biographer of Thomas D'Arcy McGee), writing on Catholic pedagogy, playing golf and tennis, and continuing his fight against the restoration of bilingual schools by local Franco-Ontarian educators. Unfortunately, his passion for Catholic education often led to renewed public skirmishes with his French co-religionists at the separate school board, particularly on his claims of their imposing unqualified teachers on the board. He was also horrified that when the board refused to stand down on maintaining bilingual schools, thereby violating Regulation 17, the Ontario government shut down the board. He blamed the trustees (notably the Francophones) for the fact that the closure forced 622 Catholic children into public schools, including 147 from his own parish, in particular St. Matthew's School. His ensuing battles with Francophone priests and leading laymen once again earned him a warning from Archbishop Gauthier not to publish articles in the secular press. When the autonomy of the board was restored, O'Gorman scrambled to retrieve the "lost" pupils and bring them back to Catholic classrooms.

Aside from these battles of language, there were happier achievements in his renewed career as a pastor and educator. In his annual reports to the bishop, he stated that he made 50 visits to parish schools every year: at least once per week during the school year. In the 1920s, O'Gorman established the Catholic University Club, which became the leading exponent for the founding of St. Patrick's College; he was also primarily responsible for inviting the Anglophone Grey Sisters of the Immaculate Conception to Ottawa, where in 1929 they founded Immaculata High School for young women. That same year, as an acknowledgement of O'Gorman's energy and dedication to Catholic education, Bishop Michael Francis Fallon of London invited him to become principal of the Summer School of Catechetics for Teachers in London.[10] A lifelong learner, O'Gorman attended a summer school in Bavaria in 1932 to learn

---

10 *Catholic Record*, May 6, 1933.

the latest methods in religious education so he could instruct teachers upon his return to the Ottawa Separate School Board. O'Gorman even worked with a Seminarians' Aid Club, which raised money so that local young men could study for the priesthood. His dedication to Catholic education appeared to be inclusive of all levels: elementary, secondary, collegiate, teacher instruction, and seminary education.

Over and above his school board activities, O'Gorman's pastoral successes were beyond dispute, as Catholics gravitated to O'Gorman's parish. Between 1914 and 1929, his flock nearly doubled in size, from 251 to 480 families. He was also the founder of the Ottawa Boys Club, the Catholic Truth Society, and the Gaelic League of Ottawa; he was an active member of Knights of Columbus Council 485 and was a vibrant presence in the St. Vincent de Paul and Holy Name societies.

In April 1933, he was rushed to the Ottawa General Hospital for an emergency appendectomy. He never recovered. He died of complications from the surgery on April 24 of that year at the age of 49. His death came as a shock; *The Ottawa Citizen* paid tribute to him as "one of Canada's most brilliant English-speaking priests." *The Catholic Record* remarked that "lay teachers profited by his instruction and caught inspiration from his burning desire to make our Divine Saviour and His teachings better known." While undoubtedly not popular in some Francophone Catholic circles, the indefatigable O'Gorman could take partial credit for the remarkable growth of Catholic education in the Ottawa area in the early 20th century. He was also the model of how the Catholic school could be energized by the creativity and dedication of the local parish priest.

Further Reading

Daniel, I.J.E. and D.A. Casey. *For God and Country: A History of the Knights of Columbus Catholic Army Huts*. NP: Knights of Columbus, 1922.

Hurtubise, Pierre, Mark G. McGowan, and Pierre Savard, eds. *Planted by Flowing Water: The Diocese of Ottawa, 1847–1997*. Ottawa: Novalis, 1998.

McGowan, Mark G. *The Imperial Irish: Canada's Irish Catholics Fight the Great War, 1914–1918*. Montreal & Kingston: McGill-Queen's University Press, 2017.

13

Mary Margaret Eleanor Williams (Mother Mary Genevieve, OSU)
Teacher of Teachers

Courtesy of the Ursuline Sisters, Chatham

When the Ontario government of James Whitney implemented the Act Respecting the Qualifications of Certain Teachers (Seath Act) in 1907, most Catholic teachers who were members of religious orders in Ontario did not have to meet the qualifications levels required of lay teachers in the province. An agreement at the time of Confederation in 1867 had permitted teacher members of religious orders to retain their qualifications as they had existed before the Dominion of Canada was created. While the grandparenting of qualifications had been intended to be applied to individuals within religious orders, in practice the orders seemed to exercise this loophole for all teachers within the order, whether or not they had been teaching or even born before Confederation. Anglophone members of the Ottawa Catholic School Board protested the qualifications of the local Francophone Christian Brothers, and took the qualifications issue to the courts of law: the government took note and prepared legislation that would force all members of religious congregations to certify according to the general norms of teacher education. Many bishops feared that in protest against having to attend Normal School with non-Catholic teachers, many sisters and brothers would retreat from the province's separate schools, return to Quebec or the United States, and thereby hasten the collapse of Catholic education in Ontario. The sisters, however, had other ideas.

Mary Margaret Eleanor Williams was born on a farm outside Chatham, Ontario, in 1871. The second youngest of seven children, she was unable to pursue her desire to study at an advanced level, and at the age of 19 decided to enter the Ursulines of the Chatham Union, a group of professed religious who valued education and had established themselves as one of the dominant teaching congregations of women religious in southwestern Ontario. Founded during the Catholic counter-reformation in Brescia, Italy, in 1535 by Angela de Merici, the Order of St. Ursula had been the first European order to establish schools in New France. From their convent headquarters in the old city of Quebec (1639), the Ursulines educated generations of young Canadian women—and, given their reputation for teaching excellence, their alumnae consisted of both Catholic and Protestant girls, such as the daughter of the Anglican Sir Robert Baldwin, Premier of Upper Canada. Their order had included some of the most prominent women religious in Quebec history, including the Quebec founder, Saint Marie de l'Incarnation.

At the invitation of Jesuit priest Jean Jaffré, the French-born and -educated Yvonne Le Bihan (Mother Xavier) came to St. Joseph's Parish in Chatham from a mission at Sault Ste. Marie, Michigan, in 1860 and became the founder of the Chatham Ursulines in the fledgling Diocese of London. Six years later, Mother Xavier and her recruits from the local Irish Canadian community established their headquarters at "The Pines," formerly the estate of Robert M. Pegley on Grand Street in Chatham. The estate would eventually become home to the Ursuline Academy as well as the mother house. In Ontario, the Ursulines focused their attention on establishing separate Catholic schools west of Toronto, notably in Tilbury, Tecumseh, Wallaceburg, Stratford, Chatham, London, and Windsor. In the process, they gradually abandoned elements of their cloistered life and became semi-cloistered so they could move more freely within the communities where their schools were located. They also became adept at making school laws and regulations work for Catholics, as noted particularly by their creating a Continuation School in their convent in Dublin in 1915 to provide secondary school courses to Catholic children living in rural Perth County. That Williams would be drawn to this order with a reputation for educational innovation in her region comes as no surprise.

In 1890, Mary Margaret Williams entered the Ursuline Convent in Chatham; three years later, she professed her vows, becoming Sister Mary Genevieve. Like most young women in Catholic religious congregations in Ontario, she learned her teaching techniques in the convent and then proceeded to teach in the separate schools run by the Ursulines, using a "letter of permission" in lieu of an official teaching certificate. In 1899, however, she attended the London Normal School as a summer student, a route that many women religious teachers would use after the passage of the Seath Act. The summer school format was convenient as it allowed teachers to keep teaching during the other months, and for professed members of religious orders it meant that the potential mingling with non-Catholic teacher candidates was kept to a minimum. Her experiences in becoming certified must have influenced her determination to make certain that other women religious were properly certified and continually developed professionally as teachers. In the early years of her career she gleaned considerable classroom experience, and by 1919 her peers in the Ursulines acknowledged her pedagogical and leadership skills by placing her in charge of seven elementary separate schools run by the sisters in Windsor.

In addition to giving her these elementary school duties, the Ursulines placed Williams in charge of what would become Glengarda Academy on Riverside Drive in Windsor. Under the watchful guidance of Mother

Genevieve, who became Superior General of the order in 1933, Glengarda Academy—originally a residence and music school for Ursulines—was transformed in 1935 into a day school and boarding school for children with developmental disabilities. This was the actualization of the dream of Sister Kathleen Taylor, an Ursuline teacher who had been working in Windsor schools with exceptional pupils. Until the passage of Bill 82 in 1980, the needs of pupils with exceptional needs were not provided for in the Ontario public school system. Thus, children with Down Syndrome or those who would now be assessed as having autism or serious cognitive disabilities were educated in private settings. Under the leadership of Sister Kathleen Taylor, with the support of Mother Genevieve, Glengarda operated as a private residential school under Ursuline leadership for most of its history, then became Glengarda Child and Family Services.

Mother Genevieve became adamant about the ongoing professional development of teachers. She developed a teacher-training curriculum that included detailed lesson planning, hands-on classroom practicums, and discussions among teachers about how the lessons had been taught and what improvements and new techniques could enhance their pedagogical skills.

According to historian Elizabeth Smyth, Mother Genevieve made certain that two basic principles were instilled in the women she trained: "Am I making thinkers of my pupils?" and "Am I teaching underlying principles in each case rather than forms and problems only?" She had many insights about effective lesson planning in all subject areas, including religion, which she freely admitted was often taught poorly. "It is so often so badly taught," wrote Mother Genevieve, "that if it were not divine doctrine, it would have been dead and buried long ago." Accordingly, she demanded that teachers meet the highest pedagogical standards, modelling the virtues, behaviours, and intellectual rigour that they demanded of their students.

Included in the ongoing education of teachers was her effort to encourage women to aspire to higher education. She actively promoted the development of programs and the academic accreditation of professors at Brescia College (called Ursuline College until 1963), the Ursuline liberal arts college for young women that was founded in 1919 in London,

Ontario, and affiliated with the University of Western Ontario. By the time she had become Superior General, the College had been operating on its campus near Western for nearly a decade. Once again drawing on her passion for education, Mother Genevieve encouraged sisters to study for their doctoral degrees and in 1936 oversaw the foundation of one of Brescia's flagship programs: Home Economics (now the Department of Food and Nutritional Science).

In many ways, the women religious of Ontario's Catholic schools have remained anonymous in the written histories of Catholic education until very recently. While her name may not have been well known across the province, Mother Genevieve was a giant in Ursuline circles and among the supporters of separate schools in the Diocese of London. She continued to serve as Superior well into her 70s. Having been a professed member of the Ursulines for 52 years, Mother Mary Genevieve died on January 3, 1946, after having a stroke. She was laid to rest in Old St. Anthony's Cemetery in Chatham, among the other deceased sisters of her order. So respected had Mother Genevieve been within her community that within five years of her death, her colleague Mother Marie Rosier, in an effort to preserve Mother Genevieve's legacy to inspire new generations of sister-teachers, wrote *Joy in the Pattern*, a biography outlining the dedicated work and thought of one of Catholic education's pioneers in teacher education.

With thanks to Dr. Elizabeth Smyth, University of Toronto, for her assistance.

Further Reading

Rosier, Mother Marie. *Joy in the Pattern: A Study of the Ursuline Life and Teachings of Reverend Mother M. Genevieve Williams, O.S.U. (1871–1946)*. Chatham: The Pines, 1951.

Skidmore, Patricia. *Brescia College, 1919–1979*. London, ON: Brescia University College, 1980.

14

John Read Teefy, CSB
Catholic School Visionary

I t may appear somewhat ironic that a man who had so much influence on Ontario's Catholic schools, from elementary to post-secondary, was not a product of them himself. John Read Teefy was born on August 21, 1848, in Richmond Hill, Ontario. The second of nine children born to Matthew and Elizabeth Teefy, John attended the Richmond Hill Grammar School and upon graduation was admitted to the University of Toronto. For four years Teefy studied classics and mathematics, earning the University's silver medal in mathematics at his convocation in 1871. He decided to enter the teaching profession, but once again, it was to the public schools that he turned, spending time as an instructor in Beamsville, Port Rowan, and at the Hamilton Collegiate. For a young man pursuing a teaching career beyond elementary schools, there were slim pickings in the Catholic community: the very few college schools in the province were run exclusively by men's and women's religious orders. In 1871, Egerton Ryerson, Ontario's Superintendent of Education, created the foundations of the secondary school system, but few Ontarians, Protestant or Catholic, pursued education beyond the eighth grade.

Despite his long association with non-denominational public education in the province, Teefy remained a fervent Catholic. His biographers claim that it was a sermon by Bishop John Farrell of Hamilton that prompted him to enter the Grand Séminaire in Montreal in 1874. True to his vocation as a teacher, Teefy joined the Congregation of St. Basil, a religious order of men founded in France. The Basilians had been serving in Ontario since 1852, after being invited to Toronto by their former pupil, Bishop Armand de Charbonnel. After spending time at St. Basil's Novitiate, located at Assumption College in Sandwich (now Windsor), Teefy professed his final vows in 1878 and joined the staff of St. Michael's College in Toronto. It would be at St. Mike's that Teefy would dedicate himself to strengthening Catholic education in Ontario and pioneering a unique partnership between Toronto's Catholic college and its large non-denominational neighbour, the University of Toronto.

There was little doubt in Teefy's mind that Catholics had more to gain by co-operating with Protestants in Ontario than by barricading themselves in a safe, sanitized bubble, pursuing their own educational path in isolation from the greater world. With the knowledge of the U of T administration, Teefy began to negotiate a partnership wherein the men at St. Michael's College could prepare for the graduating exams set by the University. Should the young men succeed in their studies and graduating exams, they would be awarded baccalaureates from U of T. In 1881, in partnership with the University's Vice-Chancellor, Sir William Mulock, St. Michael's became a formally affiliated college with the University of Toronto, with the right to set its own examinations in philosophy and history. Both of these subjects would ensure the Catholic integrity of St. Mike's graduates—particularly philosophy, which in Catholic institutions at the time was almost exclusively the scholastic philosophy of St. Thomas Aquinas. In 1910, when Teefy served as Assistant Superior General of the Basilians, his protégé Father Henry Carr effected the federation of

St. Mike's with U of T, thereby permitting St. Mike's students who had completed four years of studies there to be automatically eligible for the University's degrees, without having to register at University College. The Teefy-Carr model of federation has been replicated across Canada, creating partnerships between small Catholic colleges and larger publicly funded universities for the benefit of Catholic students. Unlike the free-standing Catholic universities of Europe and the United States (and a few exceptions in Canada), the Teefy-Carr model has been a beneficial solution for Catholics in Canada, who were a vulnerable minority outside of Quebec.

Teefy's work extended to improving the curriculum in Ontario's Catholic elementary schools. In the 1890s, it was clear to the Ontario bishops that Catholic schools, if they wanted to survive, would have to be far more competitive with their non-denominational counterparts, particularly in delivering a strong curriculum that helped students advance in their studies and enriched them in their faith. Until that time, Catholic school boards did not all purchase the same textbooks for their schools. Some boards opted for the authorized provincial texts, and some used those published by the Brothers of the Christian Schools or the Catholic books published by Sadlier's of Montreal. Some schools used a mixture of the two, or whatever was cheapest. Considering the Sadlier series pedagogically weak, the bishops appointed Teefy general editor of a new series of five readers that would serve Catholic students from form one to five (grades 1 to 10) and could be standardized across the province. In 1899, Copp Clark published Teefy's *Canadian Catholic Reader* series. It featured Canadian-oriented poems, short stories, and essays, while blending in matters pertaining to the Catholic faith: Church history, the saints, and prayers. At the beginning of the 1899 school year, London's *Catholic Record* praised Teefy's fourth reader for its "character building" quality with selections from "the best English, American and Canadian writers ... whose influence in moulding character is so great." Teachers praised the books for their superior treatment of phonics, their Catholic content, and the durability of the books themselves. Teefy's readers established a strong precedent for Catholic schools in the province to produce their own curricular materials.

The one problem Teefy and the bishops encountered was that to maintain high standards, textbooks had to be revised and republished regularly. By 1909, the bishops commissioned Teefy to review the recently revised public school readers and make recommendations on necessary revisions to the Catholic school texts. The cost of a new series, however, was prohibitive, amounting to over 60 per cent more than the cost of a set of public school readers. When the project was shut down, the bishops asked Teefy whether the public school readers could be used in the Catholic schools on an interim basis; Teefy had high praise for the public school readers, except for the "excessive militarism" in the books, which might "excite antagonism" as far as "our French Canadian citizens are concerned." With the backing of Bishops David Scollard of Sault Ste. Marie, Fergus Patrick McEvay of Toronto, Charles Hugh Gauthier of Ottawa, and Michael O'Brien of Peterborough, the old Catholic school texts would be used along with the new public school readers. Nevertheless, by the 1920s and '30s, the bishops had produced the Corona series, which replaced Teefy's Copp Clark series.

Throughout his life, Teefy busied himself as a teacher, writer, pastor, homilist, and school administrator. He served as Superior General of St. Michael's College from 1889 to 1903. During that time he wrote the first comprehensive history of the Archdiocese of Toronto, the famous *Jubilee Volume*, in 1892; one year later, he was named by Archbishop John Walsh as the first editor of the *Catholic Register*, central Ontario's weekly Catholic newspaper. Surprisingly, amidst his other duties, as if time were no object, in 1894 Teefy earned a Master of Arts degree from the University of Toronto, having written a biography of Armand de Charbonnel. Two years later, in recognition of his contributions to education and scholarship, the University of Toronto conferred on Teefy an honorary doctor of laws, and in 1906 he was appointed to the University's Senate. It was in this position that he was able to oversee the completion of the federation between St. Mike's and the University. While serving as Assistant Superior General of the Basilian Order, Teefy was diagnosed with diabetes, which ultimately took his life on June 10, 1911. In his eulogy in the St. Michael's College yearbook of 1912, the writer described Teefy as "genial in disposition, kind and charitable, a man of broad sympathies who commanded the respect and esteem of all with whom he came into contact ... no one ever formed even a slight acquaintance with him who did not feel his own character strengthened or enlivened."[11]

Further Reading

McCorkell, Edmund J. *Henry Carr: Revolutionary*. Toronto: Griffin House, 1969.

Platt, Wallace K. *Dictionary of Basilian Biography: Lives of Members of the Congregation of Priests of Saint Basil from its Origins in 1822 to 2002*. Toronto: Congregation of St. Basil and University of Toronto Press, 2005.

Shook, Laurence K. *Catholic Post-Secondary Education in English Canada: A History*. Toronto: University of Toronto Press, 1971.

---

11   Cited in Platt, *Dictionary of Basilian Biography* (1969), 154.

15

Archbishop Neil McNeil
Prophetic Voice for Justice

Courtesy of the Archives of the Roman Catholic Archdiocese of Toronto

Had his family's plan been fulfilled, Neil McNeil would have spent his life in his father's blacksmith shop in Hillsborough, Cape Breton, Nova Scotia, where Neil was born in 1851. A local schoolmaster changed Neil's life when he discovered that the young apprentice blacksmith had a natural aptitude for mathematics and a variety of other subjects. Neil and his younger brother Daniel, the son who had been intended for higher education, were sent to St. Francis Xavier College in Antigonish. Neil graduated in 1869 and began his career as a secondary school teacher in eastern Nova Scotia. It appeared education was in his DNA. In 1872, Bishop John Cameron of Antigonish sent McNeil to

Rome, where he studied theology and philosophy; five years later, he was ordained for Cameron's diocese.

Upon his return to Canada, Dr. McNeil could speak Latin, French, Italian, Spanish, and Greek, in addition to his native Gaelic and English. His rise in the local educational structures and within the Church was meteoric. After founding and editing a local newspaper, *The Aurora*, while working at St. F. X. as a professor of science and Latin, McNeil was appointed Rector of the University.

When he retired from the position after a serious falling out with Bishop Cameron in 1891, he served in a Francophone Acadian parish in Cape Breton and then was named Vicar Apostolic, later Bishop, of St. George's, Newfoundland (1895–1910). He virtually built his new diocese with his own hands, drawing on his skills as a blacksmith, stone mason, roofer, electrician, and carpenter, as churches and rectories were created in this sparsely populated frontier along Newfoundland's west coast, along the Gulf of St. Lawrence. In 1910, the Vatican transferred McNeil across the continent to another frontier, where he became the first Archbishop of Vancouver who had not been a member of a missionary religious order.

Within two years, however, the Vatican sent him to Toronto; the Archbishop there, Fergus Patrick McEvay, had recently died, leaving an unfinished legacy of education for priests, the accommodation of immigrants, and reconciliation with the majority Protestant population. McNeil arrived in Toronto in late December 1912 and immediately set to work on educational projects that would influence all of Ontario, and most notably its Catholic school system. His first priority was to complete St. Augustine's Seminary, which had been founded by McEvay, and which would train priests in the English language for most of the dioceses in Ontario and for the western mission areas. When the seminary opened in 1913, McNeil expressed the hope that this centre of priestly education "would do much to harmonize the many elements of Canada's population. Our Church and our Country are both vitally interested in securing this harmony." McNeil knew that the tens of thousands of Catholic immigrants pouring into Ontario from what is now Poland, Italy, Belgium, Malta, the Austro-Hungarian Empire, Germany, and Christian sections of the Ottoman Empire such as Lebanon would have to be accommodated by their own national parishes, their own clergy, and in the case of the Ukrainian Catholics, protection within their own distinctive Byzantine Rite.

To this end he established new parishes and recruited new priests, but just as important, he made sure that Catholic schools in his Archdiocese (which included the current Catholic school boards of Niagara, Toronto, York, Dufferin-Peel, Durham, and Simcoe-Muskoka) would provide a strong curriculum and guide "new Canadian Catholic" students into the mainstream of Ontario society—particularly its job market. "In their homes they speak a similar variety of language," commented McNeil, "but the language of the school is English and the books are Canadian. The teachers know no other language ... and the playground is English." In Catholic schools McNeil envisioned both an invigorated Church and a united citizenry of Canada. Moreover, in 1914, he became an educational reformer in his own right, investigating ways of replacing the teaching of the catechism with catechesis that would move beyond rote learning— a method that he felt produced more a "distaste for religious principles and pious practices" than a true love of the Church and the truths for which it stood. He spent much of the next 20 years trying to reform the practice of religious education in Catholic schools, with little immediate success except for the brief introduction of religious pedagogy developed by Father Roderick McEachen at the Catholic University of America.

At the end of the Great War (1914–1918), Neil McNeil realized, as did his episcopal colleagues, that the two great challenges to Catholic schools in Ontario were the lack of public funding to Catholic secondary schools and the province's inequitable distribution of corporate and business taxes. In 1871, Egerton Ryerson created the secondary school as the capstone to his educational reform project that had begun 25 years before. When Catholic educators asked for funding for their high schools, the government denied the request, stating that the British North America Act protected denominational educational rights established in law in 1867; since high schools did not exist at that time, Catholics, according to the Department of Education, had no claim on any support for these schools. This was legal hairsplitting at its finest, given the fact that the Government of Quebec had awarded substantial financial assistance to Protestant high schools as a matter of principle. While Catholics might argue that they were entitled to public funds for grades 9 and 10, which had been funded when they were included as the "fifth book" classes in the old common schools, or when in rural areas they were funded in continuation schools, this was no guarantee of securing funds for the senior grades in high schools. In 1925, McNeil rallied the bishops and prompted a separate school board in his own diocese, Tiny Township in Simcoe County, to seek a legal decision that might secure public funding for Catholic secondary schools. In the landmark case, "Tiny versus the King," the judges split along denominational lines—Protestant overruling Catholic—when they decided that the Ontario government was not obliged under Section 93 of the BNA Act to fund Catholic high schools. By 1928, the case was appealed all the way to the Judicial Committee of the Privy Council, the highest court of appeal in the British Empire. It upheld the original decision, claiming that the Ontario government had the discretionary authority over school funding, but was not constitutionally obliged to provide funding in this particular circumstance. Although McNeil's spearheading of this case appeared to be for naught, Catholic schools across the province soon discovered ingenious ways of delivering grades 9 and 10, in addition to the unfunded senior grades.

In addressing the problem of the lack of equitable distribution of corporate tax revenues to Catholic schools, McNeil and his fellow bishops took a different tack. Since the 1880s, only Catholic businesses could direct their taxes to separate schools, and it was on a voluntary basis. McNeil and the bishops sought legislation to allow for a more equitable sharing of all business tax revenue, given the labour of Catholic workers in producing wealth in Ontario's businesses and the numerous Catholic shareholders in a variety of corporate ventures across the province. McNeil approached Toronto millionaire and Catholic businessman Martin J. Quinn to head the Catholic Taxpayers' Association (CTA), a lobby group and perhaps the largest Catholic lay activist organization in the province's history. Reminiscent of the Catholic Action associations in Europe, the CTA and Quinn were influential in 1934 in securing the election of Liberal leader Mitchell Hepburn as Ontario Premier. The corporate taxation legislation ultimately failed to pass, but McNeil should be remembered for his confidence in the laity to carry on the fight for Catholic schools.

McNeil did not live to see the CTA rise and fall. He died in Toronto on May 25, 1934, at the age of 82. He was remembered fondly by Catholics, Protestants, and non-Christians alike as a friend of labour, a peacemaker, an ecumenist, an educator, and a spiritual leader. The Chief Rabbi at Holy Blossom Temple in Toronto eulogized McNeil as "a great soul, indeed a kindly and sympathetic spirit, and yet withal possessed a fine prophetic ardor for the cause of righteousness and justice." For Catholic education he was a builder of schools, a promoter of equality, and a pedagogical innovator, well ahead of his time. For the Canadian Church, he may have been one of the most impressive prelates in its history—and one of its most humble.

Further Reading

Boyle, George. *Pioneer in Purple: The Life and Work of Archbishop Neil McNeil.* Montreal: Palm Publishers, 1951.

McGowan, Mark G. *The Waning of the Green: Catholics, the Irish, and Identity in Toronto, 1887–1922.* Montreal & Kingston: McGill-Queen's University Press, 1999.

Power, Michael. *A Promise Fulfilled: Highlights in the Political History of Catholic Separate Schools in Ontario.* Toronto: OCSTA, 2002.

16

Martin Joseph Quinn
Passionate Lay Leadership

Courtesy of the Collection of Dr. Peter Meehan, Vancouver

A native of Gananoque, Ontario, Martin Quinn was born in August 1871, the oldest child of Thomas and Cecilia Quinn. When he was a teenager, he and his family relocated to Toronto, where he trained as a plumber. By the time he was 40, Quinn had built his modest plumbing business into The National Equipment Company Limited, a multimillion dollar plumbing and heating systems supplier to local building contractors. Quinn, his wife, Anne, and their nine children were active at St. Cecilia's Parish in the junction area of West Toronto, and he was a prominent member of the Toronto Board of Trade. In 1931, when Quinn attempted to direct his tax on $92,000 of his corporate stock in the Weston Company to the Toronto Separate School Board, he was flatly rejected by Weston's board of directors. Quinn publicly addressed what he considered an injustice to Catholic businessmen who wished to direct their tax support to separate schools.

In 1886, Premier Oliver Mowat amended the existing laws mandating that all businesses had to pay their taxes to the public school boards, allowing Catholics who owned their own business to redirect their taxes to Catholic schools. Where Catholics did not constitute the majority of shareholders, however, the taxes defaulted to the public board. By the 1930s, and the onset of the Great Depression, Catholic schools were desperate for all revenue streams, having depended on a very small property tax base, a meagre portion of the government's Common School Fund, reduced government funding for grades 9 and 10, no funding for senior grades, donated services from religious orders, and little or no corporation tax monies. Catholic schools faced possible extinction.

In 1931, Quinn's public advocacy for justice regarding Catholic school funding caught the eye of the seasoned education advocate Archbishop Neil McNeil of Toronto. In private conversations with Quinn, McNeil came to realize that given the bishops' and Catholic clergy's recent lack of success in advancing the cause of Catholic schools in the Tiny Township case, it might be better to motivate the laity to take leadership in the public fight for a just distribution of business and corporate taxes to Catholic schools. By 1932 McNeil had enlisted the services of leading laymen, including Quinn, to head what would become the largest mass movement of Catholics in the history of the province: the Catholic Taxpayers' Association. The new CTA executives elected Quinn as their leader and public advocate.

Mobilized in over 400 parishes across the province, the CTA enlisted ordinary Catholic parishioners to lobby the government for amendments to the Assessment Act to provide Catholic schools with a more equitable share of the corporate and business tax. As CTA branches lobbied their local members of provincial Parliament, Quinn himself led delegations to advance the case with Conservative Premier George Henry. Strategically located across the province in key ridings, the CTA became a potential political threat. While Henry's government was already extremely unpopular because of its inability to halt the worst effects of the Depression in the province, the Premier knew he could not afford to offend the strong Protestant and Loyal Orange Order constituencies that propped up his failing political machine. He delayed and waffled on amendments to the corporate tax laws favouring the public schools.

Enraged by the delays and double talk, Quinn set upon a new strategy—working with the opposition Liberals. In 1933, Quinn made a speech to the Knights of Columbus in Toronto in which he indicated that if Henry's government would not offer Catholics justice on the tax front, the quarter of a million Catholic voters would find political allies more amenable to Catholic rights. Behind the scenes, Quinn and the CTA turned to the leader of the opposition, Mitchell Hepburn, whose Liberal Party had been in the political wilderness for nearly 30 years. While there was no public agreement between the CTA and the Liberals, it became increasingly clear that there was a deal afoot between them when the province's voters headed to the polls in 1934. The election results were clear: Hepburn swept the province, and the Conservatives pointed to the CTA as the principal reason for their defeat.

Although Quinn lobbied the new Premier to live up to his private verbal agreement, Hepburn's new government was slow in delivering the promised tax bill for Catholics. The Liberals excused themselves from swift action for reasons ranging from blaming the need to delay the issue until after the federal election, to the promise of delivering a report by their investigative committee. Quinn's and Hepburn's relationship deteriorated further when, in a public speech to the Knights of Columbus in Oshawa, Quinn allegedly threatened Hepburn in a manner similar to the warning he had issued to Henry months before. Quinn denied this interpretation of his speech, but the damage was done. Nevertheless, in the spring of 1936, the amendments to the corporate tax act were successfully passed in the Ontario Legislature, on the weight of Hepburn's Liberal votes. The new act pleased neither Protestants, who rejected it on grounds that nothing more should be granted Catholic schools after the Scott Act (1863), nor Catholics, who criticized the tax allocation, which would be determined by the proportion of Catholic to Protestant shareholders in a company rather than on the actual proportion of Protestant to Catholic attendance in the local schools.

Worse, in December 1936, the province witnessed one of the most blatant sectarian political campaigns since the 19th century. With the death of the sitting Conservative MPP in East Hastings (Belleville and area), a by-election was called and the Conservatives made "special privileges" for Catholic ratepayers the issue. At the village of Plainfield, a future Conservative leader and Ontario Premier, George Drew, made an inflammatory speech about Catholics as a "conquered" people, while condemning the Liberals for the proposed corporate tax redistribution. The CTA had no powerful voice because Quinn was in Australia assisting local Catholics to advance their rights for Catholic education. The Conservatives won the riding handily; Hepburn knew he could not take the corporate tax issue to the people in the next provincial election. CTA leaders engaged in new negotiations with the government, but due to his sour relations with the Premier, Quinn could not take a lead role. The die of public opinion, however, had already been cast, and in March 1937, the Assessment Amendment Act was repealed. Hepburn himself supported repeal, decrying the bigotry he had faced from Conservatives, but personally professed his commitment to see that the Catholic minority receive economic justice in another way.

Quinn, unconvinced of Hepburn's sincerity, put CTA parish chapters on alert that the fight for their rights would continue, even if it now might be against the Liberals. By this point, however, both the lay leaders of the CTA and the bishops had lost confidence in Quinn's leadership style. He did not enjoy the confidence of McNeil's successor in Toronto, James C. McGuigan, and Hepburn refused to communicate with him directly. In January 1939, Quinn resigned from the CTA. He continued his passionate fight for Catholic schools on his own, publishing pamphlets and lobbying using his own money. He died in 1949, nearly penniless after losing investments during the Depression and spending much of his own fortune advancing Catholic education. The *Canadian Freeman's* tribute was on the mark: "To the extent that today Catholics count as well as being counted, the credit is Mr. Quinn's."

Note: The author credits the work of historians Franklin Walker and Peter M. Meehan.

Further Reading

McKenty, Neil. *Mitch Hepburn*. Toronto: McClelland and Stewart, 1967.

Meehan, Peter. "The East Hastings By-Election of 1936 and the Ontario Separate School Tax Question." CCHA *Historical Studies* 68 (2002): 105–32.

Walker, Franklin. *Catholic Education and Politics in Ontario*. Toronto: The Federation of Catholic Education Associations of Ontario, 1964.

17

Margaret Lynch
Teacher and Labour Advocate

Courtesy of OECTA

t is hard to imagine a time when Ontario's teachers were not members of bargaining units that negotiate better wages and working conditions, fight to protect job security, and seek an enhanced educational environment for their members and for those whom they teach. In the 19th and 20th centuries, however, teachers in Ontario were not well organized, and the existence of small school boards and hundreds of rural school sections ensured that teachers were generally at the mercy of what their local trustees could pay, or what ratepayers were willing to bear. Catholic teachers were subject to school boards that received little to no business tax revenue, a school rate from a small population of Catholics compared to the tax base for the public schools in the same areas, and a smaller share of provincial grants, once known as the Common School Fund. While Catholic boards benefited from the fact that teachers from religious orders donated their salaries back to the system, the problem remained that lay teachers were owed a just wage, if Catholic boards were to be in step with the social teaching of the Church. As members of religious orders declined in the 20th century, and the number of lay Catholic teachers increased across the province, it became obvious to teachers and school administrators that the status quo for Catholic schoolteachers was not sustainable.

Margaret Lynch was one such visionary who recognized that Catholic teachers would have to organize themselves more effectively, not just as a means of communication and professional development, but as a single voice to address the changes needed in Catholic education. Lynch was born in Campbellford in 1899, the eldest of four children of Daniel Lynch, a local lawyer, and Emma McKenna, an artist. As a youth, Margaret attended the local public elementary school and middle school in Campbellford (there was no separate school at the time) and then entered the Laura Miller School of Dramatic Arts. It seemed that the young Margaret was more inclined to follow the career path of her mother than of her father, although her younger sister Emily would eventually be called to the Bar of Ontario. In 1922, with few career prospects available in a slumping post-war economy, Margaret acquired a letter of permission to teach elementary school and accepted invitations to teach at St. Basil's Catholic School in Brantford and St. Patrick's School in Guelph. In 1924–1925, she attended the provincial Normal School in Peterborough and then moved to Windsor, where she spent the rest of her teaching career. Remaining unmarried, she dedicated herself exclusively to the children of the Windsor Catholic Separate School Board, teaching at eight elementary schools over her 40 years with the board.

At the beginning of her career in the 1930s, she would have noted three profound realities in the Catholic school system. First, economic depression notwithstanding, there was a wide gap between what lay Catholic teachers earned and what their colleagues in public school boards were paid. In Ottawa in 1930, for example, a Catholic teacher made, on average, $750 per year, whereas a public school teacher in the same city earned $1200. Second, it was becoming clearer by the time of

113

the Second World War that increasing numbers of lay teachers were entering the separate school system. In the 1940s, fewer than half of Catholic teachers were members of a religious order; by 1965, religious would constitute only around 15 per cent of Catholic teachers in a system that was expanding, particularly in urban areas. Third, Lynch was aware that teachers' associations were fledgling institutions. It was only in 1924 that the Ontario Teachers Council was formed as an umbrella organization for three associations: the Federation of Women Teachers of Ontario (1918), the Ontario Secondary School Teachers' Federation (1919), and the Ontario Men's Teachers Federation (1921). In 1939, Francophone teachers created a separate federation: L'Association des enseignants franco-ontariens (AEFO). Catholic teachers' associations, however, were even more rudimentary and local in their focus, with small associations in the major urban areas of Toronto, Ottawa, and Lynch's own board in Windsor. In 1943, the new provincial government under the Conservative George Drew drafted the Ontario Teacher Professions Act, which would pave the way for the creation of the Ontario Teachers' Federation (OTF). Despite his track record of being less than sympathetic to Catholics and to the development of separate schools, Drew favoured Catholic participation in the OTF. Catholic bishops and trustees both agreed that Catholic teachers should form some larger entity and have a strong voice in OTF; as a local leader among Windsor's teachers, Margaret Lynch was poised to lend her expertise to a new province-wide movement.

In February 1944, Catholic teacher-delegates from each region, sponsored by trustees and the bishops, met in Ottawa to discuss the formation of a Catholic teachers' association. Seven of the province's 11 dioceses were represented at this formative meeting. Bishop John Thomas Kidd of London appointed Lynch as one of the delegates from Windsor, and she quickly made an impression on fellow delegates. The meeting decided to create a provisional executive to work on forming an association and then hold a general meeting at Easter, later that spring. Lynch was elected provisional president. This position placed her at the heart of a drive to gather together Catholic teachers for the proposed association and to negotiate the entry of this association into the OTF. One of her first tasks was to prepare a letter addressed to all Catholic teachers advocating the forming of an association to improve the remuneration and working conditions of both religious and lay teachers in the system.

With the first general meeting scheduled at the Royal York Hotel in Toronto on April 11-12, 1944, there was little time for the provisional executive to establish a framework upon which a new Catholic teachers' union could be built. Fortunately, Lynch leaned heavily on her sister Emily, now a lawyer in Windsor, to help draft the proposed association's first Constitution. It was also helpful that the bishops and trustees were co-operative in the formation of this fledgling organization, although in retrospect, Lynch commented that the creation of a large provincially recognized association of Catholic teachers would more formally set Catholic institutions in the entire provincial education network: therefore, trustees would benefit from this stability and government recognition through additional provincial grants for teachers' salaries. The Toronto meeting witnessed the participation of nearly 600 delegates who formally established the Ontario English Catholic Teachers' Association (OECTA) to ensure justice in terms of teachers' salaries, negotiate for teachers in their separate school boards, advance the reputation of Catholic teachers in Ontario, and further the mission of the Catholic Church through its schools.

With OECTA established and Lynch confirmed as its first president, she was tasked with creating local interest in the union among teachers in separate school boards across Ontario. To this end, on a limited budget, she traversed the province by rail on weekends, was lodged through the generosity of local women religious, and met with groups of teachers. By 1945, there were 2,000 OECTA members in 21 centres across Ontario. In addition to these organizational meetings, she had to represent OECTA on the board of governors of the Ontario Teachers' Federation. There she was an advocate of a minimum salary scale for all elementary teachers, regardless of school board. She was insistent that if the government proposal of $1200 per annum per teacher was extended to elementary teachers, the package should also be made available to separate school teachers. In her mind, there should be equity of pay between all the members of OTF. "If I had agreed to the request that was submitted to me by OTF," commented Lynch, "to allow the Government of Ontario to pass a law giving a guaranteed minimum salary to teachers, but excluding Catholic teachers, we would have closed the door forever on any future opportunities and relegated ourselves to the position of second class citizens." Given the difficulties related to implementing the minimum wage, questions of teacher accreditation, and the separate school issue, the government waited to implement the proposal until the Hope Commission had filed its report on the state of education in Ontario. OECTA prepared its own scale for separate school teachers, grounded in principles of pay equity, separate from the OTF deliberations. In 1945, according to the rules of the OECTA Constitution, Lynch stepped down as president and was succeeded by Father Bernard Harrigan of Hamilton. She continued to serve as past president for one year, and then as a councillor for OECTA until 1961.

Lynch's tireless work for Catholic teachers did not go unrecognized. In 1953 she was awarded the Coronation Medal by Queen Elizabeth II to acknowledge her service to teaching and to the schools of the Windsor area. Eleven years later, in 1964, she was made a Charter Member of the Ontario Teachers' Federation. For its part, in 1968, OECTA inaugurated the Margaret Lynch Fellowship of the Study of Catechetics, an honour that is still given out annually to an outstanding Catholic teacher. In Windsor itself, the Margaret Lynch Award is given out annually to a teacher demonstrating excellence in the board. In 1969, OECTA made her an honorary member of the union she had helped to establish. She died in Windsor in 1985, having left a legacy of excellence in classroom teaching and a record of dedicated service to the teaching profession. She held the Catholic system to the values of justice, dignity, and integrity that resonate from the Church's own social teaching. The Catholic educational community in Ontario has never been the same.

Further Reading

Coo, Sheila. *The First Forty Years: OECTA 1944–1984*. Toronto: Ontario English Catholic Teachers' Association, 1984.

Dixon, Robert T. *Be a Teacher: A History of the Ontario English Catholic Teachers' Association, 1944–1994*. Toronto: Ontario English Catholic Teachers' Association, 1994.

McGowan, Mark. *The Waning of the Green: Catholics, the Irish, and Identity in Toronto, 1887–1922*. Montreal & Kingston: McGill-Queen's University Press, 1999. Chapter 4.

18

Bartley Edmund "Ed" Nelligan
Architect of a New Era

Courtesy of Toronto Catholic District School Board

n the 1960s, Catholic education in Ontario was at a crossroads. Catholic immigrants from southern and eastern Europe were entering Canada at an unprecedented rate, but many of them were unfamiliar with the province's publicly funded Catholic schools. A fresh and new generation of teachers was arriving as more and more lay men and women began teaching in separate schools, while religious orders began to decline in terms of recruits. Catholic secondary schools did not exist in the manner that most of us know them today. Grades 9 and 10 were partially funded, and grades 11 to 13 were funded privately, supported by religious orders and tuition fees. Many of these facilities were poor, with few of the curricular and program amenities that were standard in public schools. Most separate school boards were small and funded on a shoestring. What was needed in the province was innovative and creative leadership that would modernize Catholic schools without sacrificing the core Gospel values that were the animating spirit of the separate school system. Ed Nelligan was just such a leader. He would renovate and expand Ontario's largest Catholic school board, making it a model for the revolution in Catholic education in the 1980s.

Bartley Edmund Nelligan was born on March 30, 1923, in Hamilton, Ontario. Having completed his elementary and high school education in that city, he ventured to St. Michael's College, at the University of Toronto, and graduated with a baccalaureate degree in 1945. From 1946 to 1955 he served in the Hamilton Separate School Board, teaching science in the city's largest and most prestigious Catholic secondary school, Cathedral High. In 1955, he moved to Peterborough, where he assumed the position of Teaching Master at the Peterborough Teachers' College, where he taught methods of science, philosophy, and family life.

Four years later, in 1959, Nelligan became the Separate School Inspector for Peterborough and Victoria counties, a position that he held for nearly six years. The inspector reported to the Department of Education and ensured that the norms of the provincial curriculum were being maintained and that the instructional standards upheld by teachers and principals met or exceeded departmental expectations. In 1965, Edward Brisbois, the Chair of the Metropolitan Separate School Board (MSSB) in Toronto, contacted Nelligan and invited him to become the chief executive officer (director) of the board. That year the MSSB, with a student population of over 40,000, qualified under the province's new regulations to hire a Superintendent of Education. With his extensive classroom and administrative experience, Nelligan appeared to be a natural for what would be the first such position in any Catholic board in the province. Although happy with his life and work in Peterborough, Nelligan accepted the offer and, in a long-term partnership with Brisbois, transformed Catholic education in Toronto.

The board that Nelligan had come to lead was characterized by the typical array of challenges facing Catholic education across Ontario. The MSSB had been formed in 1953 and had about 55 schools. It did not control high schools, which were run entirely, as they had been for decades, by the teaching religious orders in the city: the Basilians, Christian Brothers (De La Salle), Sisters of St. Joseph, and Loretto Sisters, to name a few. The MSSB was also about nine times smaller than the Toronto public school board, which benefited from a huge base of ratepayers, full government grants, and almost all of the corporate taxes for schools in Toronto. The MSSB, meanwhile, had a small tax base with which it had to support its 52,000 students in 1963, and a very high student-to-teacher ratio. The schools themselves were old, often in poor condition, and lacking in some of the basic programs and facilities that were a fact of life in Toronto's public boards: kindergarten, libraries, gymnasia, shop and technical classes, and laboratories. The schools had been run valiantly by religious orders for over a century, but now their numbers were declining, costs were rising, and the board had not done an adequate job in recruiting children from the families of the new immigrant groups to the city. In 1951, the Catholic population of Toronto had been about 21 per cent, but with the influx of Portuguese, Italian, Polish, Ukrainian, Hungarian, Czech, Slovak, and Vietnamese Catholic newcomers, the Catholic population soared to about one third of Toronto's total by 1971. Nelligan's challenges were clear.

The new CEO and secretary of the Board (later named director) would overhaul the central administrative structure of the MSSB. He would immediately tap into the funds provided by the Ontario Foundation Tax Plan, which were provided for have-not schools in the province. He would create departments for curriculum and special services, provide funds for adult faith development for Catholic teachers, and begin an aggressive school renovation and building plan. To increase the board's "service factor" (maximizing the number of the city's Catholic children in the schools), he would initiate a campaign in the parishes to introduce new Catholic Canadians to the separate school system in an effort to recruit more children. In the 18 years following his hiring, the results confirm that Nelligan, by building effective partnerships between himself, trustees like Ed Brisbois, the Archdiocese, and local religious orders, transformed the MSSB. His spearheading of innovation in curriculum won the board the Ontario Association for Curriculum Development's Colonel Watson Award in 1978. Moreover, the Ministry of Education began to use the

MSSB for pilot projects in curriculum development and renewal. It was an asset that Nelligan's ally and friend Ed Brisbois had been appointed to the Hall-Dennis Royal Commission on Education in the mid-1960s, which gave him additional insight into the Ministry's plans to transform schools in Ontario.

The bricks and mortar face of the MSSB also changed dramatically under Nelligan. If more Catholics were being recruited into the schools, more schools would be needed, which meant more applications to the Ministry of Education for permits to build. Between 1963 and 1970, the MSSB added 550 classrooms to the board, including 40 new schools, and five additional schools when MSSB absorbed the separate school boards in Etobicoke and Mimico. Between 1970 and 1980, MSSB built 49 schools. The student population of the board also increased substantially under Nelligan, from around 52,000 at the beginning of his tenure to 94,000 by 1981. In terms of growth, education historian James Brown has reported that from 1950 to 1978, the MSSB's enrolment grew at a rate of about 529 per cent, compared to the Toronto public board's rate of 172 per cent. Nelligan's initiatives can take the lion's share of the credit for growth in the 1960s and 1970s; at the time of his retirement from the board in 1983, the MSSB was servicing 80 per cent of the Catholic children in the city.

One initiative of note during Nelligan's tenure was his effort to expand the Catholic high schools in the city. Over half of Catholic students from the MSSB's elementary schools did not pursue their studies in a Catholic high school. While grades 9 and 10 were partially funded by the provincial government, students had to pay tuition for grades 11, 12, and 13. For large Catholic families, this put a Catholic high school education out of their financial reach. Moreover, public high schools—with full funding from the province and with an exclusive right to business and corporate taxes—offered the educational amenities to ensure a young person's future. Once again, Nelligan built effective partnerships to mobilize the entire Catholic community to invest in this impoverished area of Catholic education. He partnered the MSSB with Toronto's religious orders and with Bishop Philip Pocock, who had founded the Archdiocesan High School Board in 1961. The partnership proved to be one of the most creative arrangements in the history of Catholic high schools in the province. The strategy was clearly mapped out: the Archdiocese would build an eight-room school, often a port-a-pack (a portable unit of several classrooms), on a given site (often the playground close to an existing Catholic school) near Catholic families, and the MSSB would rent it for grades 9 and 10. Having proven to the Ministry of Education that a 9-10 school was warranted in the area, and after the MSSB received funding approval, a 9-10 school was built and the old school site reverted to grades 11 to 13 under the control of the Archdiocesan High School Board. With the rental money received from the MSSB, the Archdiocese would build another school on another site, and the pattern continued. In this way Nelligan's MSSB built eight new high schools, each with a public and private section, thereby increasing Catholic student retention between junior (9 and 10) and senior (11 to 13) grades from 30 per cent in 1969 to 65 per cent in 1984.

Nelligan's influence went beyond MSSB boundaries. When the Minister of Education, William Davis, was prepared to amalgamate existing public school boards into county-wide boards and "mega" metropolitan boards, Nelligan sensed an opportunity. He joined with members of the Ontario Separate School Trustees' Association (OSSTA), represented by such luminaries as Carl Matthews, SJ, Chris Assif, Hank Lotteridge, Joe Fyfe, and Father Raymond Durocher, to advance the case that in the interests of equity, Catholic school boards should be included. In 1969, they won their case, and separate school boards were amalgamated into 63 new jurisdictions. These new mega boards, although sacrificing the subsidiarity once enjoyed by small boards, gained the advantage of increased government funding for programs, curriculum consultants, and technological resources, while creating larger bargaining units of teachers [see the chapter on Margaret Lynch]. With the creation of Catholic mega boards, separate schools were now placed on a better footing for funding, and the multiplication of budgets and resources required by the small boards was now streamlined and made more efficient.

Nelligan also played a key role in advocacy for funding completion of the Catholic system from grades 11 to 13. After failing to acquire funds for these senior secondary school grades through the "schools in need" provisions of the Foundation Tax Plan, Nelligan forged partnerships with Catholic trustees to advance the case for funding equity in Ontario education. In 1969, he was part of the team that prepared the OSSTA brief for

121

funding equity in Ontario's schools. The principles of equity unpacked in the brief won the support of both the Liberal and New Democratic parties. The governing party, however—the Progressive Conservatives under the newly minted Premier, William Davis—disagreed. They opposed funding completion during the general election of 1971, sweeping to power with 78 of 117 seats in the Ontario Legislature. It appeared the funding issue was dead. Undaunted, Nelligan and his partners, particularly Carl Matthews and Ed Brisbois, persisted, although they sometimes disagreed on the manner in which completion might be achieved. Nelligan, in partnership with now Archbishop Pocock, vowed to build one high school a year in the MSSB as proof of the need for the schools and of the government's funding folly. In 1984, with Davis's reverse of policy, and his announcement that as a matter of justice provincial funding would extend to the senior grades in Catholic high schools, the tenacity of the Catholic partners appeared to pay dividends. The Minister of Education, Dr. Betty Stephenson, created the Planning and Implementation (for funding completion) Committee (PIC), which had eight members, including three separate school representatives. Nelligan, who had just retired from the MSSB, was not only one of the three Catholic representatives, he became the PIC's vice-chair. In some ways this may have been the crowning achievement for this tireless advocate of funding completion; he was now making the dream a reality.

Nelligan had laid the foundations for a modern Catholic school system in the province with his financial, administrative, curricular, and infrastructure innovations in Toronto. It was only fitting that shortly after his retirement, the MSSB gave him its Award of Merit. In the same spirit, the Catholic Educational Association of Ontario bestowed upon him its medal of honour. In 1985, the Ontario Catholic Supervisory Officers' Association instituted the B.E. Nelligan Award of Merit, to be awarded annually to "A person who has made an outstanding and tangible contribution to Catholic Education in Ontario." Recipients of the award over the past 30 or so years read like a who's who of Catholic education in the province, particularly retired directors and superintendents of education, but also clergy and religious who have walked the path of the legacy left by Nelligan. Ed Nelligan died after a brief illness in Toronto on March 8, 2004. Acknowledging that Catholic education in the province had lost one of its giants, one of Nelligan's successor Directors of Education in that city, Tom Donovan, eulogized eloquently in the *Catholic Register* on March 28 of that year: "He was renowned for his calm confidence and generosity, and his collaborative leadership. Most importantly Mr. Nelligan was a strong and determined leader whose first priority was always the children in our schools."

Further Reading

Brown, James. "The Formation of the Metropolitan Separate School Board (Toronto), 1953–1978." In Mark G. McGowan and Brian P. Clarke, eds. *Catholics at the Gathering Place: Historical Essays on the Archdiocese of Toronto, 1841–1991.* Toronto: Canadian Catholic Historical Association, 1993. Pp. 275–91.

Dixon, Robert T. *Catholic Education and Politics in Ontario.* Vol. IV. Toronto: Catholic Educational Foundation of Ontario, 2003.

———. *We Remember, We Believe: A History of Toronto's Catholic Separate School Boards, 1841 to 1997.* Toronto: Toronto Catholic District School Board, 2007.

Power, Michael. *A Promise Fulfilled: Highlights in the Political History of Catholic Separate Schools in Ontario.* Toronto: OCSTA, 2002.

19

Anna Clare Berrigan, GSIC, Father Leo Austin, and Desmond Newman

Building Clerical, Lay, and Religious Partnerships—The Founding of Denis O'Connor Catholic Secondary School, Whitby

Courtesy of the Grey Sisters of the Immaculate Conception, Pembroke

While individuals have certainly distinguished themselves in their contributions to further the life and health of Catholic education, it is often the case that the successes and achievements within the system were the product of strong partnerships of extraordinary individuals, rather than a solitary effort. As described in the profiles of many Catholic leaders in this volume, the successful lobbying of a government, the formation of a bargaining unit, or the building of a school resulted when many talented individuals together unleashed tremendous creative energy to reach their goals. In the early 1960s, one such partnership in Whitby, Ontario, featured Father Leo J. Austin, Sister Anna Clare Berrigan, GSIC, and Desmond Newman (representing Catholic laypersons). It gave birth to a new Catholic secondary school where few thought such an enterprise would be viable.

Settled by American Loyalist and British immigrants in the early 19th century, the Town of Whitby, some 50 kilometres east of Toronto, was the county town of Ontario County, a busy Lake Ontario port and agriculture service centre for a thriving farming community stretching as far north as Lake Simcoe. Like much of its hinterland, the town was primarily Protestant; the tiny Catholic community, housed at St. John the Evangelist Church, had flipped back and forth from parish to mission status. The period between 1951 and 1961, however, was one of remarkable growth for the town, as new residents were attracted to Whitby because of its proximity to the booming automobile industry in Oshawa and various local furniture factories (Sklar Peppler) and food processing factories (Coby). In just 10 years, the Catholic population jumped tenfold, from 370 to 3701 faithful. The surging Catholic population put pressure on local church facilities, and there were new demands to build Catholic schools.

Serendipitous to this dramatic increase in Whitby's Catholic population was the arrival in 1956 of a new priest, 41-year-old Leo J. Austin. A native of Toronto, Austin was born in 1915. Ordained for the Archdiocese of Toronto in 1939, he had served in both city parishes and rural communities. He was quite simply a dynamo of energy with ideas to match; shortly after his arrival, he began a fundraising campaign to build a new church on lands owned by the Whitby Separate School Board. He became active in the building and renovation of the town's two Catholic elementary schools, co-founded Scouts and Guides for Catholic children, and was a charter member of the new Knights of Columbus Council #4895. In 1961, he approached a group of laymen, including chemist and separate school board trustee Desmond Newman, to discuss the creation of a Catholic high school for Whitby. The closest Catholic secondary schools were those in Toronto and a small high school run by the Sisters of St. Joseph in Oshawa. This religious order was already assisting at St. John's parochial school in Whitby, but lacking additional teaching sisters, they declined both continued service at St. John's school and the offer of partnership to found a Catholic high school.

Not to be sidelined by challenges, Austin called upon the Grey Sisters of the Immaculate Conception (GSIC), with whom he had worked while pastor in Midland. In 1959, at Austin's invitation, the Greys came to Whitby. They founded a convent in the old rectory and assumed control of St. John's elementary school; Austin was now living close to his new church (it opened in 1958), an architectural curiosity inspired by Austin's openness and the engineers at the Massachusetts Institute of Technology—the church building has the only inverted hyperbolic parabolic roof in Canada. In 1962, Newman, the chair of the high school committee, with Father Austin and Sister Anna Clare Berrigan of the Grey Sisters, began planning for a secondary school and prepared a brief for the Archdiocese of Toronto. Newman, with the approval of auxiliary Bishop Thomas Fulton, formally invited the Grey Sisters to found the new high school in 1963. Sister Anna Clare had professed vows in 1948 and had been teaching at O'Gorman Catholic High School in Timmins before arriving in Whitby. She became the first principal and the only teacher of a grade 9 class of 22 students, temporarily housed at St. John the Evangelist school (in 1962), close to the church. In 1963, a grade 10 class was added under the auspices of the Whitby Separate School Board, and Sister Mary Diane, GSIC, doubled the number of staff.

The formal opening of the new Denis O'Connor Catholic High School (colloquially known as DO'C) took place in 1964, adjacent to the church parking lot. The school's namesake, Denis O'Connor, CSB (1841–1911), had been born near Whitby in Pickering Township: he was a Basilian priest, distinguished educator, superior of Assumption College in Windsor, the fourth bishop of London, and the fifth bishop of

Toronto (1899–1908). In 1965, parishioners at St. John's created a private school board, with St. John's parishioner James K. Ledden as chair, to administer the senior grades at DO'C, which at the time were unfunded by the government.

The school itself was sustained by the sacrifices of all of the partners. Father Austin rented a truck and personally transported textbooks and school equipment from the recently closed Continuation School in Eganville, in the Ottawa Valley, to DO'C. Sister Anna Clare managed a growing staff consisting of members of her congregation and lay teachers, until her transfer to her native Ottawa in 1967. (There she served as principal of St. George's and Holy Rosary elementary schools, and later Immaculata and St. Patrick's high schools.) Sister Anna Clare was replaced at DO'C by Sister Mildred Moyle (Margaret Mary), who continued the Greys' commitment to educational leadership in Whitby. Catholic families like those of Des and Marjorie Newman supported the school in a variety of ways, not the least of which was through paying tuition fees for the senior grades. The community partnerships evidenced in Whitby were typical of stories of Catholics working together to build and sustain Catholic secondary schools across the province. Upon these foundations, and the 141 students registered in 1967, the tradition in Catholic education continued at DO'C, which relocated to a new building in Ajax in 1984: upon in its 50th anniversary, it supported a population of over 860 students. It is now one of seven Catholic high schools in the Durham Catholic District School Board, an amalgamation of the separate school boards in the former Ontario and Durham counties.

Father Austin retired from the parish in 1975 due to illness, and died in 1984. It was only fitting that in 1989, the Durham Catholic Separate School Board designated a new Whitby Catholic high school as Father Leo J. Austin, which marked its 25th anniversary in 2014. Sister Anna Clare continued her distinguished career in education, including four years' service at the Ontario English Catholic Teachers' Association, work with First Nations students in BC, and teaching in China. She currently lives at the Grey Sisters' mother house in Pembroke. Desmond Newman served as Mayor of Whitby from 1966 to 1975 and is still active in St. John the Evangelist Parish. Together, these three pioneers represent a model of partnership in faith and the building of community that is integral to

Catholic education. Each represented even larger groups of dedicated Catholics—clergy, religious, and laity—who saw fit to make sacrifices for a school system that was dedicated to nourishing the mind, the body, and the soul. Father Austin may have said it best when he addressed the first graduating class of DO'C in 1967: "May your spiritual goodness light up the darkness for others who choose to surround themselves with only technological knowledge while forgetting to reach out to the infinite reality."

With thanks to Mary Ruddy, GSIC, Anna Clare Berrigan, GSIC, and Desmond Newman.

Further Reading

Gidney, Robert. *From Hope to Harris: The Reshaping of Education in Ontario.* Toronto: University of Toronto Press, 1999.

"The Grey Sisters of the Immaculate Conception, GSIC." In William O'Brien, CSB, Mary Jane Trimble, CSJ, and James Mason, CSsR, eds. *Walking the Less Travelled Road: A History of the Religious Communities within the Archdiocese of Toronto, 1841–1991.* Toronto: Archdiocese of Toronto and Mission Press, 1993. Pp. 57–58.

St. John the Evangelist, Whitby, Ontario, 1883–1983. Whitby: St. John the Evangelist Parish, 1983.

20

Lorne Howcroft
Principled Principal

Courtesy of the University of St. Michael's College, Alumni & Development Office

Born in Hamilton, Ontario, on June 14, 1928, Lawrence Bernard ("Lorne") Howcroft followed a career trajectory common among young Catholic men in Ontario of his day. Having completed his elementary and secondary education in Hamilton, he attended St. Michael's College at the University of Toronto. At the time it was Canada's premier Catholic institution of higher learning, run by the Congregation of St. Basil, an order of religious noted for their intellectual life and dedication to the social teaching of the Church. After his graduation from St. Mike's in 1949, Howcroft studied for the priesthood at St. Augustine's Seminary in Toronto and was ordained, in 1953, by Bishop Joseph Francis Ryan. He was incardinated in the Diocese of Hamilton, where he served for

15 years. One of his first tasks was to obey the request of his bishop to move to Guelph and assume the position of principal of Notre Dame High School (now Bishop Macdonell) in Guelph. It did not take long for Howcroft to recognize that there were lay teachers on staff with better skill sets to run the school. In an act that demonstrated his own vision of servant leadership, he retained direct authority as principal over the grade 9 students, while unofficially delegating the principal's responsibilities over the remaining grades to laypersons with greater experience and skill than he. Such was an early example of Howcroft's leadership skills and his ability to create a respectful and co-responsible community among educators.

Throughout his teaching and administrative career, which spanned 42 years in three Catholic school boards, he soon became known for his emphasis on building community as the key to a Catholic school and on modelling concretely the values of Catholic education within the school and the community at large. Numerous teachers have testified to his ability to mentor young teachers, his deep spirituality, his skill as a team builder, his humour, and his passion for witnessing the social teaching of the Catholic Church. This grounding of all things in the faith was notable even when he helped found the Ontario Catholic High School Principals' Association, which brought together a community of administrators; this included a pledge to meet once a year at a Catholic retreat house or religious institution to remind them of their vocation as *Catholic* educators.

After leaving the priesthood in 1968, Howcroft served in several capacities in Catholic education, including as the founding principal, in 1973, of Cardinal Newman High School in the Metropolitan Separate School Board (now the Toronto Catholic District School Board). There he continued his passion for building Christian community and his emphasis that such a community be a witness for social justice. An active opponent of the Vietnam War, he interviewed and later hired an American Ph.D. student who sought Howcroft's help in avoiding conscription to the US Army. Later, in a similar act of peace advocacy, Howcroft marshalled students to protest outside the Canadian headquarters of Litton Industries when it was reported that components for American cruise missiles were going to be manufactured in Canada. On another front, he helped raise the consciousness of students in the 1990s, when Monsanto Corporation sued Saskatchewan farmer Percy Schmeiser for harvesting genetically modified Monsanto seeds that had been blown onto his farm. For Howcroft, these incidents challenged the social teaching of justice and peace that the Church had formally taught since the promulgation of the papal encyclical *Rerum Novarum* (On the Condition of the Working Class) in 1891. His witness to this application of Gospel teaching was a means of prompting students to engage in civic life and bring the Gospel to all that they do.

One story in particular highlights the effectiveness of Howcroft's ability to model Catholic education and its social advocacy, and to touch his colleagues and students deeply. In May 1984, he was principal of Cardinal Leger Catholic High School in Brampton, Ontario. Ironically, the school was a short walk from the home of Ontario Premier William Davis, who lived next door to a retired Archbishop of Toronto, Philip Pocock. Howcroft once told his friend Father James Mulligan how one of his students, Victor Morgado, happened upon the Premier one Saturday cutting the grass on his front lawn. The student stopped to chat to Davis and began to ask him why his parents had to pay their public high school taxes in addition to tuition for him to attend Leger, which was in poor physical shape at the time. By his own recollection, Davis recalled that his "political" answers to Morgado appeared unsatisfactory to the student, who continued a line of argument accusing the provincial government of being unfair. As far as the student was concerned, his parents should have the right to direct their taxes to Leger, and grades 11, 12, and 13 should be fully funded by the province. The conversation ended in a stalemate. The following Monday, Morgado told Howcroft about his encounter with the Premier. Although his principal's response was "You weren't rude to him, Victor?" Howcroft sensed that the student had been imbued with the spirit of the school, and thereafter referred to him as "The Secret Weapon in Full Funding." In an interesting coincidence, within a month of the conversation, on June 12, 1984, Davis announced funding completion for Catholic high schools in Ontario. Although one should not underestimate the powers of persuasion of Davis's friend and neighbour Pocock, nor notions of political expediency by Davis's Progressive Conservative party, Howcroft's student may have been a humble agent of change, imitating a principal who, by his own example, witnessed the application of Catholic education to those around him. It is appropriate that Cardinal Leger School annually presents the Lorne Howcroft Award to "a graduating student who has demonstrated leadership in the area of peace-making and social justice within the school community."

Howcroft's lifelong dedication to social justice did not end with his retirement in 1994. He continued to serve as a supply administrator to the Dufferin Peel Catholic District School Board and never lost sight of teaching moments with his staff and students. In 1999, several Catholic peace activists in Toronto faced criminal charges for attempting to remove a sword from inside the cross on the war memorial at Old St. Paul's Anglican Church in downtown Toronto. Activists saw the Great War Memorial's juxtaposition of the large sword on top of the cross as an affront to Christian principles of peace and Jesus Christ's invocation to love one's neighbour, including one's enemies. On the day of the activists' trial at Toronto's Old City Hall courthouse, Howcroft and his school chaplain, Brian Finamore, accompanied 150 secondary school students from Mississauga for a "day of study" at the event. The trial drew significant attention in the city and within the Catholic community, particularly because Bishop Thomas Gumbleton, Auxiliary Bishop of Detroit, testified for the defendants. During a lull in the proceedings, one of the Crown attorneys asked Howcroft why these students were not in school learning the basics. Howcroft replied, "Today's lesson, sir, is Catholic citizenship and leadership. The class *is* in session!" Apparently, his remark drew a thunderous ovation from the crowd. While such episodes that deviated from the standard curriculum and school regimen might make many school administrators wince, this was not the case with Howcroft, who understood that Catholic leaders were called to act as prophetic voices of justice and peace, grounded in their faith.

Howcroft also brought his passion for justice outside of the school setting, becoming a supporter and advocate for Romero House, a settlement house in downtown Toronto for refugees. His dedication to the project was also linked to the schools, made evident in his proposal to engage students as volunteers to assist with the resident refugees. On his urging, Romero House sponsored a volunteer internship program, in which high school students could engage in community service with some of the most vulnerable new members in Ontario society.

In 2008, the Alumni Association of St. Michael's College, Howcroft's alma mater, named him the recipient of the first Richard M. Alway Award. The award's purpose reads like the story of Lorne himself and his life's work: it is awarded to a person who "demonstrates the highest character beyond reproach, has made a significant contribution to the pursuit of spiritual, professional, and personal excellence and brings both esteem to himself and honour to the college." In many ways the award was life coming full circle for Howcroft, who had imbued the principles of his Basilian mentors at this College—"teach me goodness, discipline, and knowledge"—and then marched forth into life witnessing these principles in everything he did, both in the school and in the greater world outside of it. Lorne Howcroft died on July 26, 2014, in Brampton, Ontario, at the age of 86. He left behind his wife, Carmela, five children, and 10 grandchildren. He also left a powerful legacy of principled leadership in Catholic education and advocacy for the marginalized, for the poor, and for peace. One might truly say of him that he did not just talk the talk of Catholicism: he walked the walk and witnessed the Gospel as a teacher, a mentor, a leader, and a prophetic voice in our times.

With thanks to James Mulligan, CSC, Brian Finamore, and Joan Cronin, GSIC, for sharing their stories of Lorne Howcroft with me.

Further Reading

Brampton Gaurdian, July 31, 2014.

Dixon, Robert. "William Davis and the Road to Completion in Ontario's Catholic High Schools, 1971–1985." CCHA *Historical Studies* 69 (2003): 7–33.

Mulligan, James T., CSC. *Catholic Education: Ensuring a Future*. Toronto: Novalis, 2005.

Toronto Catholic District School Board website. https://www.tcdsb.org/schools/blessedcardinalnewman/AboutUs/SchoolHistoryAndTradition/Pages/default.aspx.

Afterword

An Examination of Conscience and a Rallying Cry

t is important that the final biography in this volume is that of Lorne Howcroft. The issues of faith and justice near and dear to Lorne ought to give us pause and prompt us to a collective examination of conscience if we consider ourselves supporters of Catholic education in 21st-century Canada.

- Have supporters been able to live up to the faith formation, sacrifice, community building, and mission of Catholic schools as modelled by the 22 people represented in this book?

- Have the teachings of the Good News, particularly the Beatitudes, been the principal catalysts animating contemporary Catholic schools, or have other things gotten in the way?

- Have supporters become imprisoned by the sometimes hollow-sounding CatholicEd-speak that is trotted out at public events, at conferences, in school board communiqués, and in a host of other forums?

- Have supporters become hostages to narrow theological perspectives? Pope Francis describes this as seeing the Church as "a sort of NGO stripped of the luminous mysticism so evident in the lives of Saint Francis of Assisi, Saint Vincent de Paul, Saint Teresa of Calcutta, and many others," or as people of faith who forget that defending the unborn is a sacred duty, but that "Equally sacred ... are the lives of the poor, those already born, the destitute, the abandoned and the underprivileged, the vulnerable infirm and elderly exposed to covert euthanasia, the victims of human trafficking, new forms of slavery, and every form of rejection" (*Gaudete et Exsultate*, nos. 100–101). A true culture of life demands that the people of God embrace together both the social and moral teachings contained in scripture and tradition.

- Have the partners in Catholic education embraced what Pope Francis has referred to, and the Ontario bishops have reiterated, as the goal of Catholic education: "to prepare hearts using the language of love, dialogue and service? … This means that as partners in Catholic education it is not about the great things we do; it is about doing little things with great love. This is the heart of joyful discipleship; it is the foundation of Catholic education." (*Renewing the Promise*, 21).

As this book goes to press, the Roman Catholic Church is facing internal stress and a crisis of Catholic identity in Rome itself. When he was elected in 2013, Jorge Bergoglio, the Cardinal Archbishop of Buenos Aires, signalled that the Church had to reform itself in the spirit of Vatican II. His taking of the name Francis, the medieval friar who bore witness to a radical holy poverty in his effort to "rebuild the Church" of his day, should have sent a powerful signal to those who preferred the status quo in today's Church. He has called for a "Church of the poor for the poor" (*Evangelium Gaudium*), for a better effort to be stewards of creation (*Laudato Si'*), and for priests and bishops who as pastors live with "the smell of the sheep" (Chrism Mass, 2013). Francis sees the Church as a "field hospital" serving humanity, a Church of the streets, and always a place of welcome and mercy. His words and witness should provide a powerful example to Ontario's Catholic schools as they navigate the social and cultural changes that have taken root in Canadian culture, and the challenging times ahead.

If Stuart Macdonald and Brian Clarke, the authors of *Leaving Christianity: Changing Allegiances in Canada since 1945*, are correct in their current assessment of the numeric and generational health of the Catholic Church in Canada—and I have no reason to doubt their analysis—the Catholic community has much work to do and many pathways for action.

The Church and its schools might opt to entrench in the status quo, ignoring the prophetic voices both within and outside of its membership. But Pope Francis calls upon the Church, and by implication Catholic schools, to take risks (General Audience, Catholic Education Congress, *Educating Today and Tomorrow: A Renewing Passion*, 21 November 2015). Partners in Catholic education might attempt a meaningful engagement with the culture around them and emulate the early Church, which sought to be leaven for the world. Such an approach might call for Catholics to listen for and seek the Spirit, who may be working in different ways, within a different set of historical circumstances, in which the status quo may be neither life-giving nor essential to the health of the Church at this moment of history.

Whatever the case, there are a great many questions facing supporters of Catholic schools in the province, especially this one: Will Catholic schools fulfill the role of being prophetic voices in our world and being the "field hospitals of the faith," as Francis beckons the Church to be? The challenges are many, but perhaps in recognizing that these schools, and Catholic education in general, have always faced challenges, contemporary school supporters might pause and recapture a sense of hope. The stories of today's "new pioneers"—chaplains, students, teachers, parents, administrators—are being lived and written all around us, if we choose to see and to hear.

Selected Bibliography

Adams, Howard. *The Education of Canadians, 1800–1867: The Roots of Separatism*. Montreal: Harvest House, 1968.

Alfred, Reverend Brother. *Catholic Pioneers of Upper Canada*. Toronto: Macmillan, 1947.

Assembly of Catholic Bishops of Ontario. *Renewing the Promise: A Pastoral Letter for Catholic Education*. Hamilton: Institute for Catholic Education, 2018.

Barber, Marilyn. "The Ontario Bilingual Schools Issue, 1910–1916." *Canadian Historical Review* 47 (September 1966): 227–48.

Bastarache, Michel. "Nos défis face á la mise en œuvre du droit de gestion des établissements scolaires à la minorité linguistique au Canada." *Éducation et Francophonie* 22 (janvier 1985): 26–33.

Beaudoin, Gerald-A. "L'arrêt Mahé, impact et conséquences." *Éducation et Francophonie* 19 (avril 1991): 4–7.

Bethune, Norman L. and Robert T. Dixon. *A Documentary History of Catholic Schools in Ontario, Vol. I: Right or Privilege? 1841–1867*. Toronto: Ontario English Catholic Teachers' Association, 1974.

———. *A Documentary History of Catholic Schools in Ontario, Vol. II: Survival? 1867–1949*. Toronto: Ontario English Catholic Teachers' Association, 1974.

———. *A Documentary History of Catholic Schools in Ontario, Vol. III: Completion? 1950–1973*. Toronto: Ontario English Catholic Teachers' Association, 1975.

Blair, Willis L. *Report of the Commission on the Reform of Property Taxation in Ontario*. Toronto: Queen's Printer, 1977.

Bordeleau, Louis-Gabriel et al. *Les Écoles secondaires de langue française en Ontario : dix ans après*. Toronto: Ontario Ministry of Education, 1980.

Bouchard, Mary Alban, CSJ, "Pioneers Forever: The Sisters of St. Joseph of Toronto and Their Ventures in Social Welfare and Health Care." In Mark G. McGowan and Brian P. Clarke, eds. *Catholics at the Gathering Place: Historical Essays on the Archdiocese of Toronto, 1841–1991*. Toronto: Canadian Catholic Historical Association, 1993. Pp. 105–18.

Boulay, Gerard. *Du Privé au Public: Les Écoles Secondaires Franco-Ontariennes á la Fin des Années Soixante*. Sudbury: Université de Sudbury, 1987.

Bowman, Lorna. "Catholic Religious Education in Ontario: Opportunities and Challenges for the 1990s—Implications for Teacher Education." *Journal of Religious Education* (Summer 1991): 362–76.

Boyle, George. *Pioneer in Purple: The Life and Work of Archbishop Neil McNeil*. Montreal: Palm Publishers, 1951.

Brown, James. "The Formation of the Metropolitan Separate School Board (Toronto), 1953–1978." In Mark G. McGowan and Brian P. Clarke, eds. *Catholics at the Gathering Place: Historical Essays on the Archdiocese of Toronto, 1841–1991*. Toronto: Canadian Catholic Historical Association, 1993. Pp. 275–91.

Cameron, David R. and Graham White. *Schools for Ontario: Policy Making, Administration and Finance in the 1960s*. Toronto: University of Toronto Press, 1972.

Careless, J.M.S. *Brown of the Globe*. Vol. 1: *The Voice of Upper Canada, 1818–1859*. Toronto: MacMillan, 1959.

———. *Brown of the Globe*. Vol. II: *Statesman of Confederation, 1860–1880*. Toronto: Macmillan, 1960.

———. *The Pre-Confederation Premiers: Ontario Government Leaders, 1841–1862*. Ontario Historical Studies Series. Toronto: University of Toronto Press, 1975.

Cecillon, Jack. "Turbulent Times in the Diocese of London: Bishop Fallon and the French Language Controversy, 1910–1918." *Ontario History* (December 1995): 250–89.

Choquette, Robert. "English-French Relations in the Canadian Catholic Community." In Terrence Murphy and Gerald Stortz, eds. *Creed and Culture: The Place of the English-Speaking Catholic Church in Canada, 1750–1930*. Montreal & Kingston: McGill-Queen's University Press, 1993. Pp. 3–24.

———. *La Foi : Gardienne de la Langue en Ontario, 1900–1950*. Montreal: Bellarmin, 1987.

————. *Language and Religion: A History of French-English Conflict in Ontario*. Ottawa: University of Ottawa Press, 1975.

————. "The Archdiocese of Toronto and Its Metropolitan Influence in Ontario." In Mark G. McGowan and Brian P. Clarke, eds. *Catholics at the Gathering Place: Historical Essays on the Archdiocese of Toronto, 1841-1991*. Toronto: Canadian Catholic Historical Association, 1993. Pp. 297–311.

Churchill, Stacey. "Franco-Ontarian Education: From Persecuted Minority to Tolerated Nuisance." In Hugh Oliver, Mark Holmes, and Ian Winchester, eds. *The House that Ryerson Built*. Toronto: Ontario Institute for Studies in Education, 1984.

Clarke, Brian and Stuart Macdonald. *Leaving Christianity: Changing Allegiances in Canada since 1945*. Montreal & Kingston: McGill-Queen's University Press, 2017.

Coo, Sheila. *The First Forty Years, OECTA 1944-1984*. Toronto: Ontario English Catholic Teachers' Association, 1984.

Costello, Bride, IBVM. *Life and Letters of Rev. Mother Teresa Dease*. Toronto: McClelland, Goodchild and Stewart, 1916.

Curtis, Bruce. *Building the Educational State: Canada West, 1836-1871*. London: Althouse Press, 1988.

Daly, James. *Education or Molasses? A Critical Look at the Hall–Dennis Report*. Hamilton: McMaster University Press, 1979.

Dickinson, Greg. "Toward 'Equal Status' for Catholic Schools in Ontario: The Supreme Court of Canada Examines Constitutional Issues." *Canadian and International Education* (November 1987): 5–23.

Dixon, Robert T. *Be a Teacher: A History of the Ontario English Catholic Teachers' Association, 1944-1994*. Toronto: Ontario English Catholic Teachers' Association, 1994.

————. *Catholic Education and Politics in Ontario*, Vol. IV. Toronto: Catholic Educational Foundation of Ontario, 2003.

————. *Guardians at the Gates of Wonder: A History of the Huron Superior Catholic District School Board and Its Predecessor Separate School Boards*. Sault Ste Marie, ON: HSCDSB, 2012.

————. *We Remember, We Believe: A History of Toronto's Catholic Separate School Boards, 1841 to 1997*. Toronto: Toronto Catholic District School Board, 2007.

————. "William Davis and the Road to Completion in Ontario's Catholic High Schools, 1971–1985." CCHA *Historical Studies* 69 (2003): 7–33.

Dooley, Ann. "D'Arcy McGee, Fenianism, and the Separate School System in Ontario." In Robert O'Driscoll and Lorna Reynolds, eds. *The Untold Story: The Irish in Canada,* Vol. 1. Toronto: Celtic Arts of Canada, 1988. Pp. 501–20.

Fiorino, Pasquale. "The Nomination of Bishop Fallon as Bishop of London." CCHA *Historical Studies* 62 (1996): 33–46.

French, Goldwin S. "Egerton Ryerson and the Methodist Model for Upper Canada." In Neil McDonald and Alf Chaiton, eds. *Egerton Ryerson and His Times.* Toronto: Macmillan, 1978.

Gaffield, Chad. *Language, Schooling, and Cultural Conflict: The Origin of the French-Language Controversy in Ontario.* Montreal & Kingston: McGill-Queen's University Press, 1987.

Galvin, Martin J. "The Jubilee Riots in Toronto, 1875." Canadian Catholic Historical Association *Report* 26 (1959): 93–107.

Gérin, Odile. *D'un obstacle á l'autre : vers le Conseil scolaire de langue française.* Ottawa: Les Éditions L'Interligne, 1998.

Gidney, Robert. *From Hope to Harris: The Reshaping of Education in Ontario.* Toronto: University of Toronto Press, 1999.

————— and W.P.J. Millar. *Inventing Secondary Education: The Rise of the High School in Nineteenth-Century Ontario.* Montreal & Kingston: McGill-Queen's University Press, 1990.

Godbout, Arthur. *L'origine des écoles françaises dans l'Ontario.* Ottawa: Les presses de l'Université d'Ottawa, 1972.

————. *Nos écoles franco-ontariennes.* Ottawa: Les presses de l'Université d'Ottawa, 1980.

Hall, Mr. Justice E.M. *Living and Learning: The Report of the Provincial Committee on Aims and Objectives of Education in the Schools of Ontario.* Toronto: Queen's Printer, 1969.

Henderson, E.F., et al. *Historical Sketch of the Separate Schools in Ontario and the Catholic Separate School Minority Report.* Toronto: The English Catholic Education Association of Ontario, 1950.

Higgins, Michael and Douglas Letson. *My Father's Business: A Biography of His Eminence G. Emmett Cardinal Carter.* Toronto: Macmillan, 1990.

Hill, Philip G. *Ontario Catholic Education and the Corporate Sector: A Report Submitted to the Institute for Catholic Education*. Toronto: Institute for Catholic Education, 1997.

Hodgins, J. George. *Documentary History of Education in Upper Canada, from the Passing of the Constitutional Act of 1791 to the Close of Dr. Ryerson's Administration of the Education Department in 1876*. 28 volumes. Toronto: L.K. Cameron, 1894–1910.

————. *Legislation and History of Separate Schools in Upper Canada*. Toronto: William Briggs, 1897.

Houston, Susan E. and Allison Prentice. *Schooling and Scholars in Nineteenth Century Ontario*. Ontario Historical Studies Series. Toronto: University of Toronto Press, 1988.

Humphries, Charles W. *"Honest Enough to Be Bold": The Life and Times of Sir James Pliny Whitney*. Ontario Historical Studies Series. Toronto: University of Toronto Press, 1985.

Lahr, D.A. and R.D. Gidney. "Who Ran the Schools? Local Influence on Education Policy in Nineteenth Century Ontario." *Ontario History* (1972): 131–43.

Lei, Christine. "Material Culture at the Loretto School for Girls, Hamilton, 1861–1971." CCHA *Historical Studies* 68 (2000): 92–113.

McGowan, Mark G. *The Imperial Irish: Canada's Irish Catholics Fight the Great War, 1914–1918*. Montreal & Kingston: McGill-Queen's University Press, 2017.

————. *Michael Power: The Struggle to Build the Catholic Church on the Canadian Frontier*. Montreal & Kingston: McGill-Queen's University Press, 2005.

————. "What Did Michael Power Really Want? Questions Regarding the Origins of Catholic Schools in Canada West." CCHA *Historical Studies* 68 (2002): 85–114.

————. *The Waning of the Green: Catholics, The Irish, and Identity in Toronto, 1887–1922*. Montreal & Kingston: McGill-Queen's University Press, 1999.

McKenty, Neil. *Mitch Hepburn*. Toronto: McClelland and Stewart, 1967.

Meehan, Peter. "The East Hastings By-Election of 1936 and the Ontario Separate School Tax Question." CCHA *Historical Studies* 68 (2002): 105–32.

Miller, J.R. "Anti-Catholicism in Canada: from the British Conquest to the Great War." In Terrence Murphy and Gerald Stortz, eds. *Creed and Culture: The Place of English-speaking Catholics in Canada, 1750–1930*. Montreal & Kingston: McGill-Queen's University Press, 1993. Pp. 25–48.

Moir, John S. *Church and State in Canada West: Three Studies in the Relation of Denominationalism and Nationalism, 1841–1867*. Toronto: University of Toronto Press, 1959.

———, ed. *Church and State in Canada, 1627–1867: Basic Documents*. Carleton Library Series, no. 33. Toronto: McClelland and Stewart, 1967.

———. "The Origins of the Separate School Question in Ontario." *Canadian Journal of Theology* 5 (1959): 105–17.

Mulligan, James T., CSC. *Catholic Education: Ensuring a Future*. Toronto: Novalis, 2005.

Murphy, Dennis. *Catholic Education at the Crossroads*. Toronto: *Catholic Register*, 2001.

Murphy, Michael F. "Catholic Schools for Catholic Children: The Making of the Roman Catholic School System in London, Ontario, 1850–1871." CCHA *Historical Studies* 63 (1997): 59–79.

Nicolson, Murray. "Bishop Charbonnel: The Beggar Bishop and the Origins of Catholic Social Action." CCHA *Historical Studies* 52 (1985): 51–66.

———. "Irish Catholic Education in Victorian Toronto: An Ethnic Response to Urban Conformity." *Histoire sociale—Social History* 17 (November 1984): 287–306.

———. "Michael Power, the First Bishop of Toronto, 1842–1847." CCHA *Historical Studies* 54 (1987): 27–38.

Norman, Marion, IBVM. "Making a Path by Walking: Loretto Pioneers Facing the Challenges of Catholic Education on the North American Frontier." CCHA *Historical Studies* 65 (1999): 92–106.

Power, Michael. *Jesuit in the Legislative Gallery: A Life of Father Carl Matthews, SJ*. Welland: NP, 2005.

———. *A Promise Fulfilled: Highlights in the Political History of Catholic Separate Schools in Ontario*. Toronto: OCSTA, 2002.

Prang, Margaret. "Clerics, Politicians, and the Bilingual Schools Issue in Ontario, 1910–1917." *Canadian Historical Review* 41 (October 1960): 281–307.

Rea, J.E. *Bishop Alexander Macdonell and the Politics of Upper Canada*. Ottawa: Ontario Historical Society, 1974.

Sissons, C.B. *Church and State in Canadian Education*. Toronto: Ryerson Press, 1959.

Smyth, Elizabeth, ed. *Changing Habits: Women's Religious Orders in Canada.* Ottawa: Novalis, 2007.

———. "Christian Perfection and Service to Neighbours: The Congregation of the Sisters of St. Joseph, Toronto, 1851–1920." In Elizabeth Gillan Muir and Marilyn Fardig Whiteley, eds. *Changing Roles of Women within the Christian Church in Canada.* Toronto: University of Toronto Press, 1995. Pp. 38–54.

———. "The Culture of Catholic Women's Colleges at the University of Toronto, 1911–1925." CCHA *Historical Studies* 70 (2004): 111–30.

———. "'Developing the Powers of the Youthful Mind': The Evolution of Education for Young Women at St. Joseph's Academy." CCHA *Historical Studies* 66 (2000): 114–31.

———. "Gertrude Lawler and St. Joseph's Academy: Alumnae, Advocate and Author." CCHA *Historical Studies* 72 (2006): 124–41.

Stafford, Joe. "Strict Neo-Thomism in the Catholic High Schools of the Archdiocese of Toronto, 1940–1960." CCHA *Historical Studies* 83 (2017): 47–66.

Stamp, Robert M. *The Schools of Ontario, 1876–1976.* Ontario Historical Studies Series. Toronto: University of Toronto Press, 1982.

Walker, Franklin. *Catholic Education and Politics in Upper Canada.* Toronto: The Federation of Catholic Education Associations of Ontario, 1955.

———. *Catholic Education and Politics in Ontario.* Toronto: The Federation of Catholic Education Associations of Ontario, 1964.

———. *Catholic Education and Politics in Ontario III: From the Hope Commission to the Promise of Completion.* Toronto Catholic Education Foundation of Ontario, 1986.

Wilcox, Michael. "'To meet more perfectly the wants of our people': The Christian Brothers and the Process of Anglicization in Ontario, 1850–1925." CCHA *Historical Studies* 79 (2013): 57–78.

Wilson, David A. *Thomas D'Arcy McGee.* Vol. 2: *The Extreme Moderate, 1857–1868.* Montreal & Kingston: McGill-Queen's University Press, 2011.

Young, Mary Bernita, CSJ. *Silent Growth: The Life and Times of Sister Bernard Dinan.* Toronto: Sisters of St. Joseph Historical Publications, 1986.

Zucchi, John, ed. *The View from Rome: Archbishop Stagni's 1915 Reports on the Ontario Bilingual Schools Question.* Montreal & Kingston: McGill-Queen's University Press, 2002.

Index

Anglican Church, 13, 47, 59, 132
  and John Strachan, 42
  Robert Baldwin a member, 93
Austin, Father Leo J., 124–8

Beatitudes, 135
Belcourt, Napoléon-Antoine, 82–7
Berrigan, Sr. Anna Clare, GSIC, 124–8
Bill 30, 9
Bill 160, 29
Blair Commission, 28–9
Board amalgamation, 28, 121, 127
Bourget, Bishop Ignace (Montreal), 41
Briand, Bishop Jean-Olivier (Quebec), 16,
  35–8
Brisbois, Edward, 118, 119, 120, 122
British Empire, 16, 36, 63, 78
  and Judicial Committee of the Privy
  Council, 23, 75, 105
  Order of, 89
  and Protestantism, 37, 40
British North America Act, 1867 (BNA
  Act), 22, 23, 26, 30, 52, 61, 65, 68, 75,
  104, 105 (see also Constitution Act,
  1982)
Brothers of the Christian Schools (De
  LaSalle Christian Brothers), 51, 52, 74,
  93, 99, 119
  in Kingston, 77
Brown, George, 60, 64, 65

Cardinal Leger Catholic Secondary School
  (Brampton), 131–2
Carleton, Sir Guy (Governor), 36, 37
Carleton County, 83
Catholic Record (London), 91, 99

Catholic Register (Toronto), 100, 123
Catholic Social Teaching, 32, 113, 116, 129,
  130, 131
  *Guidelines for Business Partnerships in
  Catholic Education*, 32
  Rerum Novarum, 131
Catholic Taxpayers' Association (CTA), 25,
  105–6, 108, 109, 110 (see also taxation)
Catholic Women's League, 81
Charbonnel, Bishop Armand de (Toronto),
  21, 49–53, 54, 68, 98, 100
Clarke, Brian P., 13, 136, 13fn, 14fn
Collins, Cardinal Thomas (Toronto), 43
Common schools, 21, 23, 42, 51, 52, 59,
  65, 105
  Act (1841), 41
  Board, 42
  Grant or fund, 52, 60, 108, 113
  tax, 52, 61
Completion (of funding), 17, 31, 62, 121,
  122, 131
Confederation, (1867), 10, 22, 23, 60, 65, 92
  as a cultural pact, 84, 85
  and Indigenous Residential Schools, 26
  and minorities, 22, 81
  and teacher qualification, 92, 93
  and the Tiny Township case, 23
Congregation of St. Basil (Basilians), 52, 98,
  100, 119
  Denis O'Connor a member, 126
  at St. Michael's College, 98, 129, 133
Congregation of the Sisters of St. Joseph
  (CSJ), 18, 51, 54, 55, 56, 119
  in Oshawa, 126
  in St. Catharine's, 55

Congregation of St. Ursula (Ursulines), 18, 93, 96
   at Brescia College, 80, 95
   in Chatham, 93–4
   Glengarda, 94–5
Conservative Party (Progressive Conservative Party), 11, 60, 61, 65, 70, 86, 109, 110
   introduce Bill 30, 29
   George Drew leads, 110, 114
   George Henry leads, 108
   James P. Whitney leads, 79, 84
   and John A. Macdonald, 59, 60, 61, 65, 68, 83
   and William Davis, 29, 122, 131
Constitution Act, (1982), 10
   Section 93, 15
   and BNA Act, 30, 52
Continuation school, 23, 94, 105, 127
Council of Trent, 12

Davis, Premier William, 29, 121, 122, 131
Dease, Mother Teresa, IBVM, 44–8
Department of Education, 18, 24, 27, 47, 73, 104, 118
   and MSSB, 120–1
   as Ministry of Education, 28, 30, 119, 120–1
Dinan, Sr. Bernard, CSJ, 54–7
Drew, Premier George, 110, 114

English Catholic Education Association of Ontario (ECEAO), 28
Evangelium Gaudium, 136

Facilities (Catholic school), 25, 26, 28, 29, 31
   inadequate, 73, 117, 119
Fallon, Bishop Michael Francis OMI (London), 77–81, 83, 84, 90
Ferguson, Premier G. Howard, 85, 86
Fifth Book, 23, 105
Fleming, Sr. Gertrude, IBVM, 45, 46
Fort William (Thunder Bay), 39, 45, 49
Francophones, 24, 74, 78, 79, 84, 89, 90, 91, 93
   as teachers, 114
French Canadian Education Association of Ontario (ACFEO), 79, 83, 84, 85

Full funding, 11, 17, 33, 119, 120, 131
   and Hope Commission, 27
Fully Alive, 31

Gaudete et Exsultate, 136
Gaudium et Spes, 12
Globe (Globe & Mail), 9, 10, 53fn
   and Clear Grits, 60
   eulogizes James White, 72
   on Separate School Bill, 65
Grattan, J.D., 74
Great Depression, 25, 108, 110, 113
Grey Sisters of the Immaculate Conception (GSIC), Pembroke, 18, 95
   in Whitby, 126–7
Guelph, 113, 130
   and Loretto Sisters, 47

Hall-Dennis Royal Commission, 120
Hamilton, 26
   and Bishop John Farrell, 98
   and Convention of Separate School Teachers (1878), 73
   Diocese of, 53, 56, 129
   and Father Bernard Harrigan, 116
   and Sisters of St. Joseph, 55, 57
Hepburn, Premier Mitchell, 25, 105, 109, 110
High schools, 23, 28, 29, 31, 62, 69, 70, 81, 104, 105, 119, 120, 131
   in Brampton, 131
   in Guelph, 130
   in Ottawa, 127
   in Toronto (MSSB), 119–22, 130
   in Whitby, 126–7
Hope, Justice Andrew, 11, 26
   Commission, 27, 116
   minority report, 27–8
Howcroft, Lorne, 129–33, 135
Humanae Vitae, 12

Institute for Catholic Education (ICE), 30, 32
Irish Catholics, 21, 45, 51, 89
   clergy, 80
   and famine, 40, 45, 50, 55
   Fenians, 65–6
   and imperialism, 89
   and nationalism, 70, 78, 81

political engagement of, 59, 64–65
in schools, 65

Judicial Committee of the Privy Council,
23, 75, 105

Kidd, Bishop John T. (London), 114
Kindergarten, 11, 24, 27, 29, 119
in Francophone schools, 86
Knights of Columbus, 91, 109, 126

Laudato Si', 136
Legislative Assembly (Canada), 21, 22, 50,
59, 64
of Ontario, 61
and Scott Act, 60
and Taché Act, 21
Liberal Party, 11, 60, 61, 70, 110, 122
as Clear Grits, 60
and George Brown, 64
and Martin J. Quinn, 109
Mitchell Hepburn leads, 25, 105, 109
and Napoléon Belcourt, 83, 85
Oliver Mowat leads, 68, 69
Linguistic conflict, 20, 24, 79, 80, 85, 89
Liturgy (Roman Catholic), 11, 12, 13
London
and Assumption College, 81, 126
and Brescia College, 80, 95–6
diocese of, 53, 56, 80
and Loretto Sisters, 47
and Michael F. Fallon, 78–9
Normal School, 94
St. Peter's Seminary in, 80
and Sisters of St. Joseph, 55
and Ursuline Sisters, 93–4
Loretto Sisters (Institute of the Blessed
Virgin Mary, IBVM), 18, 42, 45, 46, 47,
48, 73, 119
Loyal Orange Order, 7, 70, 80, 84, 85, 100
Loyalty (Catholic), 21, 36
Lynch, Archbishop John Joseph (Toronto),
22, 55, 56, 67–71, 73
Lynch, Margaret, 112–6, 121

Macdonald, John Alexander, 59, 60, 61, 65,
68, 83
Macdonald, Professor Stuart, 13, 13fn,
14fn, 136

Macdonell, Bishop Alexander (Upper
Canada/Kingston), 20, 41, 130
Many Gifts, 31
Matthews, Carl SJ, 121, 122
McGee, Thomas D'Arcy, 17, 22, 63–6, 90
McNeil, Archbishop Neil (Toronto), 24, 75,
85, 102–6, 108, 110
Media literacy, 13, 32–3
and Marshall McLuhan, 33
Merchant, Dr. F.W., 80, 84
report, 85
Methodists, 59
Metropolitan Separate School Board,
Toronto (MSSB), 118, 119, 120–2, 130
Morgado, Victor, 131
Mowat, Premier Oliver, 68, 69, 73, 108
Mulligan, James CSC, 131, 132

Nelligan, Bartley Edmund "Ed", 117–23
New Democratic Party (NDP), 11, 122
Newfoundland, 38, 103
Catholic schools in, 15, 30
Newman, Desmond, 124–8
Niagara, 55, 56
Loretto Sisters and, 47
Our Lady of the Angels (NY), 68
Sisters of St. Joseph in, 55
Notwithstanding Clause, 10

Oblates of Mary Immaculate (OMI), 27,
77, 78
O'Gorman, Father John Joseph, 89–92
Ontario Catholic School Trustees'
Association (OCSTA) (see Trustee)
Ontario English Catholic Teachers'
Association (OECTA), 28, 115–6
Ontario Teachers' Federation (OTF), 114,
115, 116
Open access, 9, 31
Oshawa, 39, 45, 49, 56, 109, 125, 126
Ottawa, 59, 63, 64
and Archbishop Charles Hugh Gauthier,
100
diocese of, 68
Immaculata High School in, 90
Normal School, 75
Ottawa Catholic School Board, 85, 86, 89, 91
school board troubles, 24, 74, 85, 89, 93
University of Ottawa, 77, 78, 86, 88

Pastoral Constitution on the Church and the Modern World (*Gaudium et Spes*), 12

Pembroke, 57, 86
and Grey Sisters, 127

Peterborough, 57
and Bishop Michael O'Brien, 100
Normal School, 113, 118

Pius IX (Pope), 50, 68

Pius X (Pope Saint), 79

Pocock, Archbishop Philip (Toronto), 120, 122, 131

Pontbriand, Bishop Henri-Marie (Quebec), 36

Pope Francis, 13, 135, 136, 137

Population increases (Catholic), 22, 49–50, 80, 120, 125
baby boom, 25–6
and service factor, 119

Power, Bishop Michael (Toronto), 39–43, 45, 49–50, 51
and Loretto Sisters, 45–6

Power, Michael (historian), 14

Presbyterians, 13, 59, 69

Proselytism, 10, 12, 21, 51

Pyne, R.A. (Minister of Education), 75, 79

Quebec, 38, 93, 104
bishops of 16, 35, 37
Church in, 13, 36–7, 40, 41, 74
Irish in, 45
minorities in, 65, 81, 99
religious orders of, 75, 93
schools, 30
and the United Province of Canada, 20, 22, 50, 59, 65

Quebec Act (1774), 37, 38, 64

Quinn, Martin J., 17, 105, 107–11

Ratepayers, 10, 69, 73, 110, 112
Anglophone, 74
under Day Act, 59
under Taché Act, 59, 60
in MSSB, 119

Regulation 17, 24, 80, 84, 85, 86, 89, 90

Religious orders, 17, 18, 23, 27, 39, 42, 47, 52, 68, 92, 119, 120
decline of, 26, 113, 117
donated services, 23, 27, 108, 113

in high schools, 98, 119
qualifications of, 73, 74, 75, 94

Renewing the Promise, 136

Residential Schools (Indigenous), 26–7

Ryerson, Egerton, 21, 22, 29, 40, 42, 43, 47, 51, 52
and secondary schools (1871), 98, 104

St. Michael's Cathedral (Toronto), 50, 51, 55, 70–1

St. Michael's College, University of Toronto (St. Mike's), 15, 52, 98, 99, 100, 118, 129, 133

St. Michael's Hospital (Toronto), 55

Saskatchewan, 10, 61
Percy Schmeiser, 131

Sault Ste. Marie, 39, 57, 93
Bishop David Scollard, 100

Scott, Ian, 62

Scott, Sir Richard William, 58–62, 65, 68

Scott Act (1863), 21, 55, 58, 60, 61, 65, 68, 109

Seath Act (1907), 75, 92, 94

Second Vatican Council (Vatican II), 11, 33, 136, 12fn

Section 93 (BNA Act), 15, 22, 33, 52, 61, 65, 75, 105

Society of Jesus (Jesuits), 27, 42, 93

Strachan, John (Anglican Bishop of Toronto), 42

Taché, Etienne, 52

Taché Act (1855), 21, 52, 68

Taxation, 17, 22, 23, 25, 29, 30, 52, 60, 84, 104, 105, 131
business/corporate tax, 25, 69, 107, 108–10, 112, 119–20
Catholic Taxpayers' Association (CTA), 25, 105, 108–10
Common School Tax, 52
Foundation Tax Plan, 28, 119, 121

Teachers, 14, 15, 18, 26, 27, 29, 31, 32, 42, 52, 68, 73, 75, 90, 104, 117, 118, 137
(*see also* OECTA; *see also* OTF)
"85 Factor", 11
associations, 114, 115, 121, 127
and Bill 160, 29–30
conventions of, 73
and curriculum, 42, 99

Francophones, 85
and media, 32, 33
payment of, 25, 28, 112, 113, 114, 115
student–teacher ratio, 119
teachers' college, 23
training, 14, 42, 61, 72, 73–4, 75, 84, 86,
90–1, 93, 95, 116, 119
women religious, 56, 74, 75, 92, 94, 95,
113, 114
Teefy, John R. CSB, 97–100
Television, 8
Term 17 (Newfoundland), 15
Textbooks, 31, 73, 79, 84, 99, 100, 104, 127
Sadlier's, 99
Canadian Catholic Readers, 72, 74, 99
Timmins, 126
Tiny Township case, 23, 24, 81, 105, 108
Toronto, 26, 107, 119, 120
Knights of Columbus, 105
Normal School, 68, 73
St. Augustine's Seminary, 80
Toronto Catholic District School Board,
130
Toronto Savings Bank, 50
Toronto Separate School Board, 107
(*see also* MSSB; *see also* St. Michael's
College)
Treaty of Paris (1763), 36
Trustee, 14, 29, 52, 69, 70, 74, 112, 114, 115,
119, 121, 126
and Bill 160, 29
and language, 90
Ontario Catholic School Trustees'
Association, 14
Ontario Separate School Trustees'
Association, 28, 121
in Ottawa, 74
in Scott Act, 60
in Taché Act, 21, 52
Truth and Reconciliation Commission, 27
Tuition, 11, 23, 28, 42, 117, 120, 127, 131

Upper Canada (1791–1841), 20, 38, 41,
59, 93
Catholic minority in, 22, 65
Catholic schools, 21
United Church of Canada, 13
United Nations, 33
United Province of Canada (1841–1867),
20, 26, 50, 59
United States of America, 55, 59, 64, 75, 85,
93, 99
and anti-Catholicism, 64
University of Toronto, 6, 13, 96, 97, 98, 100,
118, 129

Walker, Franklin, 27, 110
Whitby, 18, 124–8
and Durham Catholic District School
Board, 127
White, James Francis, 17, 72–6
Whitney, Premier James P., 24, 75, 79, 84,
92
Williams, Mother Mary Genevieve OSU,
92–6
Windsor (Sandwich), 39, 42, 49, 55, 56, 73,
78, 80, 81, 83, 94, 95, 113, 114
and Assumption College, 81, 98, 126
Windsor Catholic Separate School Board,
113